So Help Me God

So Help Me God

THE FAITH OF AMERICA'S PRESIDENTS

John McCollister

Westminster/John Knox Press
Louisville, Kentucky

973.099
M13

Book design by Publisher's WorkGroup

Published by Westminster/John Knox Press
Louisville, Kentucky

This book is printed on acid-free paper that meets
the American National Standards Institute Z39.48 standard.
∞

PRINTED IN THE UNITED STATES OF AMERICA
2   4   6   8   9   7   5   3   1

Library of Congress Cataloging-in-Publication Data

McCollister, John.
    So help me God : the faith of America's presidents / John McCollister.
        p.   cm.
    Includes index.
    SUMMARY: Describes the religious backgrounds of the presidents of the United States and reveals their religious preferences while in office.
    ISBN 0-664-25210-9

    1. Presidents—United States—Religious life. [1. Presidents—Religious life.] I. Title.
E176.M147 1991
973'.0992—dc20
[B]   91-35600

Contents

Foreword

The United States of America is not a Christian nation in the strict sense. It has been called that, and the dominant religion from the beginning has been Christianity. But the founders of the republic were careful not to create either a "religious state" or a "state religion."

However, the United States does have spiritual roots. The major concepts on which its governmental structures stand are derived from the Bible. In an age when people were "subjects" and the "divine right of kings" was taken seriously, government of the people, by the people, and for the people was a radical idea, grounded in the biblical view of humanity and its value and destiny.

Columbus named the first land he discovered San Salvador (Holy Savior) and testified that he would never have found it had he not been guided by his Savior and Lord.

The Mayflower Compact and the earliest documents organizing the colonies all acknowledged divine sovereignty in their beginnings. Anglicans settled in Virginia, Puritans in New England, Quakers in Pennsylvania, and Catholics in Maryland. When the time came to decide whether to be loyal to the king of England or to become independent, the leaders in Williamsburg called for a day of prayer. Every year since the

Continental Congress, one day has been set aside as a day of prayer. Every President of the United States has proclaimed days of prayer.

The Declaration of Independence based its principles on spiritual beliefs. "We hold these truths to be self-evident, that all men are created equal [and] that they are endowed by their Creator with certain inalienable rights. . . ." Each signer of the Declaration of Independence stood silently for a moment of prayer before affixing his signature to the document.

In George Washington's first inaugural address, the thinking of the earliest American citizens is clearly stated:

> Such being the impressions under which I have, in obedience to the public summons, repaired to the present station, it would be peculiarly improper to omit in this first official act my fervent supplications to that Almighty Being who rules over the universe, who presides in the councils of nations, and whose providential aids can supply every human defect, that his benediction may consecrate to the liberties and happiness of the people of the United States a Government instituted by themselves for these essential purposes, and may enable every instrument employed in its administration to execute with success the function allotted to his charge. In tendering this homage to the Great Author of every public and private good, I assure myself that it expresses your sentiments not less than my own, nor those of my fellow citizens at large less than either. No people can be bound to acknowledge and adore the Invisible Hand which conducts the affairs of men more than those of the United States. Every step by which they have advanced to the character of an independent nation seems to have been distinguished by some token of providential agency; and in the important revolution just accomplished in the system of their united government the tranquil deliberations and voluntary consent of so many distinct communities from which the event has resulted cannot be compared with the means by which most governments have been established without some return of pious gratitude along with a humble anticipation of the future blessings which the past seems to presage. These reflections, arising out of the present crisis,

have forced themselves too strong on my mind to be suppressed. You will join with me, I trust, in thinking that there are none under the influence of which the proceedings of a new and free government can more auspiciously commence.

It is simply impossible to imagine the United States without strong and deep spiritual roots. The First Amendment to the Constitution is itself a witness to the seriousness with which biblical faith was taken.

Our earliest citizens demanded the freedom to worship God as their consciences directed and were careful to guard that fundamental freedom. The so-called separation of church and state was not a license to ignore religion but a testimony to its importance in their lives. Freedom *of* religion ought never to be confused with freedom *from* religion.

Richard C. Halverson
Chaplain, U.S. Senate

Introduction

"I have learned that Chester A. Arthur is one man and the President of the United States is another."

—*Chester A. Arthur*

"So help me God."

Four innocent-sounding, monosyllabic words, but with them forty men ceased for a time to be private citizens.

These simple prayerlike words were added, unexpectedly, to his prepared oath of office by General George Washington on April 30, 1789. They have been repeated by every successor, transforming each individual into a focal point of American history: the President of the United States.

In a land without dictators or a monarchy, these forty men have approached deification, for this is the only office in America in which the name of a person is guaranteed immortality. Every President has known who he is and, eventually, where he fits into history.

"So help me God."

From the moment of uttering those words, the new President shapes history. Whatever the President says or does is observed, monitored, and recorded by the press and then served up on a platter to an American public hungry for such news.

On the one hand, we Americans pride ourselves as independent, self-determined individuals; on the other hand, we allow ourselves to be influenced by so-called "presidential patterns." Remember? President Kennedy disliked wearing hats, and our nation's hatters suffered a major setback. President Eisenhower made golf extremely popular. President Reagan made jelly beans fashionable. And, of course, President Bush has us debating the value of broccoli.

We might look down our noses at the Hollywood gossip columnists, yet we perk up our ears for news about some facet of a President's personal life and habits—including religious faith. If the President attends church service, we want to know about it. If the President does not attend, we want to know that, too.

In a sense, it's a no-win situation. The President who seldom attends public worship is branded an infidel; the President thought to attend too often is accused of "parading" his religion.

Some critics suggest that it would be better for the President not to support religion at all, pointing to the Constitution's demand for a separation of church and state. But did the founders of our nation ever perceive an America separated from God? Would they have discouraged any Chief Executive from sharing the faith of others? Certainly not. Their theistic concept appears in the Declaration of Independence itself, which refers to Almighty God no less than four times.

In short, our country was founded as a God-centered nation. Among the President's other herculean burdens is the requirement to carry on this tradition.

The following pages describe how these temporary residents of the eighteen-acre plot at 1600 Pennsylvania Avenue expressed the deepest of all human feelings—personal religious faith. Throughout these accounts, one common note rings clear: Whatever any Chief Executive did or said became subject to public criticism.

Could it be that we Americans expect from our President a moral perfection impossible for the rest of us to attain?

PRESIDENTIAL SEAL

GEORGE WASHINGTON

George Washington

FIRST PRESIDENT, 1789–1797

"It is impossible to account for the creation of the universe, without the agency of a Supreme Being. It is impossible to govern the universe, without the aid of a Supreme Being. It is impossible to reason without arriving at a Supreme Being. If there had been no God, mankind would have been obliged to imagine one."

He was the "macho man" of the eighteenth century.

Traditional historians may chafe at this description of him; nonetheless, were George Washington living today, he would be a leader of men, a heartthrob of women, and an idol of teenagers.

The story of every nation is peppered with examples of people who respond like hypnotized sheep to the personification of power. The United States is no exception. No man was ever so powerful in his era, or perhaps in any other period of history, than the so-called father of our country. His imposing stature (six feet two inches tall, one hundred seventy-five pounds), coupled with his uncanny political savvy, made him the ideal candidate to weld the people.

As commander-in-chief of the Continental Army, General George Washington succeeded in turning back the British chiefly because he was able to keep the military forces of the thirteen colonies united. After the War for Independence, President George Washington had to reunite the citizens and transform them into "one nation under God."

Once the cord to Mother England was broken, the real problems began. The trust of one citizen for another had long since waned. Now inflation spiraled, and international trade was disrupted. Coping with newly won freedom was a greater hurdle than gaining it. Something, or someone, had to organize and direct the nation through the infant stage of an experiment called democracy.

The call went out, and George Washington was elected President by unanimous vote of the Electoral College.

One of Washington's officers, Henry "Light Horse Harry" Lee, summed up the feelings of the nation about its first President: "First in war, first in peace, and first in the hearts of his countrymen."

He would have been less than honest were he to have added "first in his church." George Washington, the man whose rhetoric influenced the masses, did not talk openly about his religious heritage. He remained an Episcopalian throughout his life and worshiped regularly at Christ Episcopal Church in Alexandria, Virginia. Nevertheless, as a result of his conspicuous silence in terms of any endorsement of the Episcopal faith, he was considered—at least by some observers—a deist, an agnostic, even an atheist.

President Washington quite probably could have stifled this gossip with a strong statement about his Christian convictions. Certainly, the Christian community and its influential clergymen would have welcomed this. Yet the political climate of the eighteenth century was unique, and the new President was willing to act and speak within the boundaries set by the times for the sake of the country.

The embryonic nation was smarting from a war that many of its citizens chose not to endorse. Contrary to popular belief, not every able-bodied man rushed to the front for a chance to fire a musket at the redcoats. In reality, on April 19, 1775, when the Revolutionary War began with "the shot heard round the world," at least a fourth of the colonists supported England.

After four years of fighting and the surrender of the British at Yorktown, bitterness and hatred still seethed in America's own backyards between Patriots and Loyalists. Tensions mounted daily. People lacked confidence. They groped for the right way, eager to follow a leader who could give them a sense of direction. The battle was no longer with a foreign principality, it was an internal strife marked with struggles for power that threatened the essential need for unity.

Where was the church in all of this? Unfortunately, it did little if anything to curb dissension. Perhaps both clergy and lay people feared that a mingling of church and state would invite problems akin to those of other countries, in which the church became the main political force. Meanwhile, some religious zealots added fuel to the existing fires of uneasiness and insecurity by crying out against "foreign Catholics," and No POPERY banners flew in parts of New England. Sermons on the potential dangers of electing "papal loyalists" to public office were preached by pastors from their pulpits; "Heaven help us," they warned, if a Roman Catholic were to be elected President.

George Washington was well aware of this anti-Catholic frenzy. He knew, too, that religious persecution often generated civil wars, and that the new nation could not survive another conflict. In his role as commander-in-chief, and again as President of the United States, he insisted on the uninhibited freedom of religious expression.

This was not a new problem for the dynamic leader. As General of the Continental Army, Washington tried to curtail expressions of anti-Catholicism. He wrote many letters to denominational leaders of Baptist, Presbyterian, Methodist, Quaker, and Dutch Reformed churches. "Religion and Morality are the essential pillars of Civil Society," he often noted. He urged them all to respect one another and to strive, as did he, to be "a faithful and impartial patron of genuine, vital religion."

In a letter written to a general convention of the Episcopal Church in 1789, Washington wrote, "The liberty enjoyed by the people of these States, of worshiping Almighty God agreeably to their consciences, is not only among the choices of their blessings, but also of their rights."

Mindful of his personal influence in such matters, George Washington was careful to avoid anything that hinted of partiality on his part, to the point that he even refused to partake of Holy Communion in the Episcopal Church once the American Revolution began. Consequently, his religious pronouncements and actions, which were broad in scope, caused some of his critics to question openly whether or not he was a Christian—using their definition of the term "Christian," of course.

This is not to say that President Washington was a "closet Christian" who smothered his real beliefs under a blanket of secrecy just to ensure unity among his people. He was diametrically opposed, for example, to the prevailing Calvinistic teaching that humans were, by nature, sinful beings whose utter dependence upon Almighty God was necessary for salvation. He firmly believed in the ultimate goodness of humanity, a goodness that was, as he wrote in a letter dated May 26, 1789, "particularly necessary for advancing and confirming the happiness of our country."

On the other hand, every once in a while, without apparent reservation, George Washington publicly called for a measure of blessings from Almighty God. For instance, at his first inauguration on Thursday, April 30, 1789, with Vice President–elect John Adams and others, General George Washington walked out onto the balcony of Federal Hall in New York City to the sound of a thunderous ovation from the thousands of people—most of whom had waited for hours—who were jamming the street below. Suddenly, the crowd became quiet as General Washington turned toward Judge Robert R. Livingston and placed his left hand on an opened Bible sitting upon a table beside him. He raised his right hand, and swore to "faithfully execute the office of the President of the United States." There was a pause. Then the President boldly added his own words: "I swear, so help me God."

A murmur rushed through the crowd and the inaugural party. This was not part of the oath of office (although every President, since, has adopted it). Finally, Washington bent over and kissed the Bible. Another murmur. Justice Livingston turned to the crowd below and cried out, "Long live George Washington, President of the United States!" People cheered. Church bells pealed. Cannons at the fort fired a salute.

After a few moments the President went inside to deliver his inaugural address, after which he and other officials were to ride in a carriage to St. Paul's Chapel at Fulton Street and Broadway for a religious service. But because most of the crowd remained on the streets, the President suggested that they walk the seven blocks to hear prayers offered by Episcopal Bishop Samuel Provoost, who had just been named Chaplain of the Senate. This was the *only* time that a religious service was an official part of a presidential inauguration.

President George Washington was an unconventional man for an unconventional age. Although he was dearly loved by the people (The *Philadelphia Journal* said in 1777, "Had he lived in the days of idolatry, he would have been worshiped as a god"), he adopted an image unlike that of any other national leader of his time. He was neither a dictator nor a monarch. Instead, he assumed a different kind of role—as protector and servant of the people. His chief obligation was not to himself but to the citizens of these United States. For him, as exemplified even through his religious expressions, personal wishes were far down his list of priorities as compared to his obligations as President. The office, according to President Washington, was greater than the man filling it.

It was a legacy that, in years to come, would benefit some of his successors . . . and prove to be the downfall of others.

JOHN ADAMS

John Adams

SECOND PRESIDENT, 1797–1801

"I have been a churchgoing animal for seventy-six years, and this has been alleged as proof of my hypocrisy."

—*Letter to Dr. Benjamin Rush,*
August 28, 1811

Although John Adams was Vice President for eight years, his name was never a household word. Owing in part to President Washington's strong personality, Mr. Adams played only minor roles in the national political scene; consequently, it was not until he was elected President that people became curious about personal matters such as his faith.

"Ask me not whether I am Catholic or Protestant, Calvinistic or Arminian," Adams said. "As far as they are Christians, I wish to be a fellow disciple with them all."

Compared with the solid convictions of his predecessor, Adams's testimony was woefully shallow. For one who had studied for the holy ministry during his college days, such a vague statement seems out of character. However, during his study at Harvard, young Adams, under the instruction of the brilliant scientist Dr. John Winthrop, expressed growing doubts about his Christian convictions. It was not long before he felt "not made for the pulpit." Finally, he abandoned all thoughts of serving a parish, pursuing instead a degree in law that led him into the political arena as a delegate to the First Continental Congress, member of the Massachusetts legislature, envoy to France and the Netherlands, minister to Great Britain, and first Vice President of the United States.

John Adams was a scholarly man whose mastery of the language left no doubt as to where he stood on any issue. Nevertheless, it is difficult to compartmentalize his religious beliefs.

On the one hand, as he admitted to his friend Dr. Benjamin Rush, "I have been a churchgoing animal for seventy-six years." On the other, Adams was not a professing Christian; he was a Unitarian whose religious convictions allowed him to continue the quest for a unified nation begun by George Washington.

Most historians agree that one of the reasons for the successful unification of the new nation lay in the fact that each of its first four Presidents were, for all practical purposes, deist (Washington, Jefferson, Madison) or unitarian (Adams). Because of the distrust among the traditional denominations of the Christian church, the essential unity necessary for the survival of this infant nation would have never been realized had an ardent Baptist, Presbyterian, Methodist, or Dutch Reformed believer been elected as Chief Executive. In a nation of religious diversity and fervor, neutrality in government was the only way to ensure peace on earth.

John Adams certainly showed no partiality toward any of the conventional denominations. Instead, he often chided the mainline churches for their unwillingness to rise from the mire of outdated teachings. "Even since the Reformation, when or where has existed a Protestant or dissenting sect who would tolerate iniquity?" he asked his friend John Taylor in a letter dated 1814. "The blackest billingsgate, the most ungentlemanly insolence, the most yahooish brutality is patiently endured, countenanced, propagated, and applauded. But touch a solemn truth in collision with a dogma or sect, though capable of the clearest proof, and you will soon find you have disturbed a nest, and the hornets will swarm about your legs and hands and fly into your face and eyes."

At times, however, John Adams spoke and wrote as though

he was at least sympathetic toward the beliefs of mainline Christians. This eldest son of a church deacon once described Christianity as "the brightest of the glory and the express portrait of the character of the eternal, self-existent, independent, benevolent, all powerful, and all merciful creator, preserver, and father of the universe, the first good, and first fair."

On December 27, 1816, he wrote, "Jesus is benevolence personified, an example for all men."

In one of his diary entries, he described the Christian religion as "above all the religions that previously existed in ancient or modern times."

America's struggle for freedom occupied Adams's waking hours. Courtship and marriage fell far down his list of priorities, until one day he met a spirited seventeen-year-old who was reading John Locke's *Human Understanding*, an exceptionally challenging bit of philosophy.

"My, what a big book for such a little head," he said.

Without so much as looking up, Abigail Smith replied, "Even a little head longs for knowledge."

"Then what do you see as our purpose on earth?" asked Adams.

The clergyman's daughter answered pointedly. "Men and women are here to serve God and humanity. We are accountable to God for every moment of our time. We are made in the image of God, and we must fulfill our promise or we are a blasphemy to God. An hour wasted is an hour's sin."

During their fifty-four years of marriage (which he himself described as a "love feast"), Adams often said of his wife, "She makes me so happy! No sour-faced girl who makes everyone feel sad, her Christian beliefs make her ever a joy to know."

John Adams, who served one term as President, was the first Chief Executive to live in what would come to be known as the White House. It might be said that it was he who left the most noticeable mark of his religious conviction as a guideline for each of the occupants who followed. Above the fireplace in the President's formal dining room is inscribed the prayer written by the nation's second President:

> "I Pray Heaven to Bestow
> the Best of Blessings on
> THIS HOUSE
> and on All that shall hereafter
> Inhabit it. May none but Honest
> and Wise Men ever rule under this Roof!"

After his defeat for reelection by Thomas Jefferson in 1800, John Adams retired from public life to study history, philosophy, and religion. Through a strange twist of fate, both Adams and Jefferson died on July 4, 1826—the fiftieth anniversary of America's independence.

THOMAS JEFFERSON

Thomas Jefferson

THIRD PRESIDENT, 1801–1809

"I have sworn on the altar of God eternal hostility against every form of tyranny of the mind of men."

—*Campaign speech, 1800*

During his years as President, Thomas Jefferson frequently worshiped with the congregation of Christ Episcopal Church, which met for services in a small, abandoned tobacco warehouse at New Jersey Avenue and B Street, S.E., below Capitol Hill.

One Sunday morning, as Jefferson was crossing an open field near the Capitol, a large red prayer book under his left arm, a stranger stopped him and asked where he was going.

"To church," Jefferson replied.

The man burst out laughing and said, "Why, Mr. President, you don't believe a word of it."

"Sir," Jefferson answered, "no nation has yet existed or been governed without religion. I, as the Chief Magistrate of this nation, am bound to give it the sanction of my example. Good morning, sir." And he marched off as the stranger, open-mouthed, gazed after him.

It is ironic that the President, vilified variously during the scurrilous campaign of 1800 as a deist, atheist, and agnostic, should have taken such a strong stand regarding the importance of religion to our nation. For, in fact, many constituents wrote him off as an atheist.

During that presidential race, a staunch supporter of incumbent John Adams (Jefferson's opponent) posed a biting question to the voters: "Do you believe in the strangest of paradoxes—that a spendthrift, a libertine, or an atheist [all referring, of course, to Jefferson] is qualified to make your laws and govern you and your posterity?"

Some historians insist on squeezing Jefferson into the mold of traditional Christianity. But to do so would be an injustice to everything Jefferson believed. He had never joined a Christian congregation. His religious views generally echoed eighteenth-century deism, which we might equate with modern-day Unitarianism, rather than those of mainline Christian denominations. Yet much of his early education was Christian oriented. His parents—Peter and Jane Randolph Jefferson, of Albemarle County, Virginia—were devout Anglicans. When he was only nine years old he went to live with the Reverend Douglas A. Scott, a dedicated Calvinist, who taught the young Jefferson Latin, Greek, and French. He attended a school run by the Reverend James Maury, a descendent of the Huguenots, in nearby Charlottesville.

But it was as a college student at William and Mary that Jefferson shaped his thinking about humankind and God. It was here, Jefferson confessed, "I got my first views of the expansion of science and of the system of things in which we are placed."

During his college days, young Jefferson showed signs of distrusting organized religion. He had a growing conviction that clergymen were corrupting the pure and simple message of Jesus.

This is not to imply that Jefferson had nothing to do with the organized church. While he was President, Jefferson not only attended Christ Episcopal Church but every New Year's Day he sent a note with fifty dollars to the rector, the Reverend Andrew J. McCormick.

Our third President was sensitive to the charge that he was opposed to the teachings of Christianity. In a letter to his friend Benjamin Rush, Jefferson asserted his religious beliefs as being "the result of a life in inquiry and reflection and . . . very different from the anti-Christian system attributed to me by those who know nothing of my opinions. To the corruptions of Christianity I am indeed opposed, but not to genuine precepts of Jesus himself. I am a Christian, but I am a Christian in the only sense in which I believe Jesus wished anyone to be, sincerely attached to his doctrine in preference to all others, ascribing to him all human excellence, and believing that he never claimed any other."

Thomas Jefferson considered himself a disciple of Jesus, although not in the sense endorsed by most of the clergy of his day. He did not accept the deity of Jesus, a basic dogma of Christianity. Nonetheless, he admired Jesus' simple teachings.

In 1815 he published a compilation of Jesus' quotes in a small volume containing passages from the four Gospels. He titled his work *The Life and Morals of Jesus of Nazareth.* Today it is often referred to as *The Jefferson Bible.*

Jefferson, who started the book during moments of relaxation while President, wrote his old friend Charles Thomson telling him how it came into existence:

> I have made a wee little book which I call the philosophy of Jesus. It is the paradigm of his doctrines, made by cutting the texts out of the book and arranging them on the pages of a blank book, in a certain order of time and subject.
>
> A more beautiful or precious morsel of ethics I have never seen. It is a document in proof that *I* am a *real Christian* [underlined by Jefferson in the original], that is to say, a disciple of the doctrines of Jesus.

The sometimes caustic Jefferson believed that Jesus' simple, straightforward teachings had been corrupted over the years by his devoted followers. In an 1820 letter to William Short he referred to Paul as "the first corruptor of the doctrines of Jesus."

The simple teachings of Jesus reflected Jefferson's attitude about such things as worship. He did not seem comfortable in cathedrals. Instead, he felt religion was "a concern purely between God and our consciences." He shaped his personal theology through a set of rather rigid principles, as would Aristotle or any of the other ancient philosophers who were his heroes. Those principles showed little patience toward anyone who would prohibit freedom of thought or conscience. "I will never by any word or act," he promised, "bow to the shrine of intolerance or admit the right of inquiry into the religious opinions of others."

He was especially critical of clergymen "who have so much abused the pure and holy doctrines of their master, and who have laid me under no obligations of reticence as to the tricks of their trade."

In his home state of Virginia, for example, the Anglican Church enjoyed such a strong influence that other denominations were hard pressed to survive. Jefferson strongly objected to this preferred status. Hence, he sponsored a Bill for Religious Freedom that said, in part, "No man shall be compelled to frequent or support any religious worship, place, or ministry whatsoever . . . but all men shall be free to profess, and by argument to maintain, their opinions in matters of religion."

Jefferson's religion was subjective, a personal relationship with the Creator. "There is only one God and he is all perfect," he wrote, "and to love God with all thy heart and thy neighbor as yourself is the sum of religion."

Jefferson was one of our country's true Renaissance men. The Virginian's political accomplishments are widely known: author of the Declaration of Independence, member of the Continental Congress and the Virginia House of Delegates, Governor of Virginia, Secretary of State under Washington, Vice President under John Adams, and President for two terms.

He was preeminent in other fields, as well. He designed Monticello, along with other buildings in Virginia, and became known as "the father of our national architecture." Jefferson also was the first major American art collector; he was president of the American Philosophical Society (which then meant scientific speculation and investigation); he was a genuine scholar, with more than a cursory knowledge of Greek, Latin, French, Italian, and Spanish; he was the first American statesman to foster public education; and he was the founder of the University of Virginia. At the College of William and Mary he studied law with Professor George Wythe from 1760 to 1762. He was admitted to the bar five years later.

Into every generation comes someone who embodies the word "genius." Thomas Jefferson was such a person. Respected historians such as Dr. Hilmar Grimm, professor emeritus of Ohio's Capital University, claim that part of Jefferson's genius lay in his ability to see beyond the moment. He could have gained political strength by aligning himself with any of the traditional churches of his day. But of more importance to him was providing an opportunity for thinking men and women to structure their own beliefs—and fate.

Perhaps that is why Jefferson did not regard attaining the presidency of the United States as his top achievement. He showed what he deemed important when he wrote the epitaph that marks his grave at Monticello: AUTHOR OF THE DECLARATION OF INDEPENDENCE, OF THE STATUTE OF VIRGINIA FOR RELIGIOUS FREEDOM, AND FATHER OF THE UNIVERSITY OF VIRGINIA.

JAMES MADISON

James Madison

FOURTH PRESIDENT, 1809–1817

"In the Papal System [Roman Catholic], Government and Religion are in a manner consolidated, and that is found to be the worst of Government."

—*1832*

He was too small to make the team. As a schoolboy in Port Conway, Virginia, young James Madison could not compete successfully in events that required athletic prowess. The man who would have the dubious distinction of becoming our shortest President (he stood five feet four inches tall and weighed under one hundred pounds) sought, instead, to make his mark in life in the tamer arena of academics, which included some formal study of the Bible and other religious teachings.

After earning a B.A. degree from Princeton in 1771, this diminutive youth, whom Washington Irving described as "a withered little apple-johnny," remained on campus for another year studying Hebrew and ethics and seriously considered the idea of entering the ministry. Although this thought was short-lived, Madison read books on theology for relaxation, a practice he continued throughout his adult life.

As was the case with most youngsters raised in colonial Virginia, Madison was schooled in the teachings of the Anglican Church. At the same time, even while he was a student, he insisted strongly on the separation of church and state, something he vigorously supported when he helped frame the Constitution of the United States.

Carrying his conviction to its logical conclusion, Madison was one of the few elected officials who opposed the establishment of a chaplain for the Congress. In 1811, as President, he vetoed an act of incorporation of an Episcopal church in the District of Columbia; he felt that such an intrusion violated the Constitution's First Amendment regarding the establishment of religion.

In the Bill of Rights for the State of Virginia, of which he was the primary author, he wrote, "Religion, or the duty we owe our Creator, and the manner of discharging it, can be directed only by reason and conviction, not by force or violence; and, therefore, all men are equally entitled to the free exercise of religion according to the dictates of conscience."

However, Madison studied theology and, on occasion, acknowledged the presence of Almighty God. In his first inaugural address in 1809 he confessed that the power of Almighty God "regulates the destiny of nations." Yet his cousin, Episcopal Bishop James Madison, observed, "His religious feelings died a quick death."

Like his predecessor and personal idol, Thomas Jefferson, Madison remained silent concerning his opinions about established religion, and he and his wife, Dolley, a Quaker, periodically attended St. John's Episcopal Church in Washington. However, his only genuine interest in the organized church surfaced when some issue threatened the separation of church and state. Then he became so outspoken on this point that the more conservative Calvinists of his day concluded that the President was "anti-church."

Perhaps the underlying reason for his constant hammering away on this theme lay in the fact that Madison was raised in an environment of sophisticated Virginians who supported only the Anglican tradition and openly discriminated against the Baptist, Presbyterian, and Congregational fellowships

St. John's Protestant Episcopal Church, across Lafayette Square from the White House. More Presidents have worshiped here than in any other church in the capital city. Courtesy St. John's Episcopal Church.

through fines, imprisonments, and banishments. This, he felt, was a sacrilege.

Once, when Patrick Henry introduced legislation to tax the public for the support of religious teaching, Madison retorted, "If this freedom be abused, it is an offense against God, not against men. To God, therefore, not to man, must an account be rendered." As a postscript, he added, "In this country is forever extinguished the ambitious hope of making laws for the human mind."

President Madison was not a staunch churchgoing Christian, to be sure. But he did all he could to ensure that others could be, if they wished it.

JAMES MONROE

James Monroe

FIFTH PRESIDENT, 1817–1825

"When we view the blessings with which our country has been favored, those which we now enjoy, and the means which we possess of handing them down unimpaired to our latest posterity, our attention is irresistibly drawn to the source from whence they flow. Let us, then, unite in offering our most grateful acknowledgments for these blessings to the Divine Author of All Good."

—*Second annual message to Congress, 1818*

The religious conviction of President James Monroe is best classified as "decision by indecision." His public religious observance, his marriage, and his funeral all took place in the Episcopal Church. No records that we have offer any evidence that Mr. Monroe rejected the Anglican faith, but at the same time we have no record that he endorsed it, either.

As indicated by his lopsided victories in 1816 and 1820, James Monroe reflected the feelings of the nation. The Revolutionary War was history, and the country wanted to settle down, relax, and grow a bit. Monroe was the ideal candidate. He didn't rock the boat, he did his job without any great fanfare, and he maintained this attitude in terms of his personal faith, never trumpeting his religious convictions.

Although President Monroe attended St. John's Episcopal Church during his two terms in office, he was conspicuous by his silence about his religious beliefs. "Religion," he said, "is a matter between our Maker and ourselves." As a result, aside from occasional passing references in his formal speeches— including both inaugural addresses—he seldom mentioned the Lord at all.

A long-time friend of President Monroe, Judge E. R. Watson

of Virginia, thought of him as a good man because, as he put it, "I never hear him use an oath or utter a word of profanity."

Even the judge had to rule solely on the basis of lack of evidence.

JOHN QUINCY ADAMS

John Quincy Adams

SIXTH PRESIDENT, 1825–1829

"I have made it a practice for several years to read the Bible through in the course of every year."

—*Diary entry of September 26, 1847*

Like father, like son.

Because John Quincy Adams also expressed his religious beliefs in different words, some members of the organized church branded him an atheist, and he thereby received from his political enemies many of the same slings and arrows as did his father, our second President. Yet this did not appear to cause anxiety, for, like his father's, John Quincy Adams's faith was a personal relationship between himself and his God.

This was no lame excuse. Throughout his life, Adams maintained a practice of reading at least three chapters of the Bible each day. The astute Ralph Waldo Emerson observed many years later, "No man could read the Bible with such powerful effect, even with the cracked and winded voice of old age." Like his father, John Quincy Adams was not a large man (he was five feet seven inches tall), so he devoted himself to academic pursuits, studying poetry (he published a book of poems in 1831), the writings of Shakespeare, the classics, and the Bible.

In spite of his obvious love of scripture, we have no record that a Bible was present when he took his oath of office on March 4, 1825. If this is true, John Quincy was the only President not to use one. However, in his inaugural address in

1825, he did end by quoting from Psalm 127: "Knowing that 'except the Lord keep the city, the watchman waketh but in vain,' with fervent supplications for his favor, to his overruling providence I commit with humble but fearless confidence my own fate and the future destinies of my country."

As to attendance at public worship, it is safe to conclude that this was not always one of Mr. Adams's practices. While serving as Secretary of State, he wrote about this fact in his diary entry of October 24, 1819. "Since I have now resided in Washington, I have not regularly attended at any church . . . chiefly because, although the churches here are numerous and diversified, not one is of the Independent Congregational class to which I belong, the church to which I was bred, and in which I will die."

Later, however, Adams changed his approach. Frank E. Edington, historian of Washington's New York Avenue Presbyterian Church, records that, while he was President, Adams served as a trustee and attended worship there more often than many of those on the membership rolls. On several occasions, according to Mr. Edington, the President loaned substantial sums of money to the congregation in order to defray current bills.

The presidential years were not particularly kind to Adams. "I can scarcely conceive a more harassing, wearying, teasing condition of existence," he said. Consequently, some of his rare moments of contentment were found while sitting in church. "Hope in the goodness of God, reliance upon his mercy in affliction, trust in him to bring light out of darkness and good out of evil are the comforts and promises which I desire from public worship," he said. "They help to sustain me in the troubles that are thickening around me."

Adams was not what you would call a popular President. Often setting principle above party, he spoke out strongly about controversial issues such as slavery. Pro-slavery forces called him "the madman from Massachusetts." Eventually, he made so many enemies that he lost his bid for reelection in 1828.

Two years later, however, he returned to Washington as a representative of his neighbors of Braintree (now Quincy), Massachusetts, and used the political platform for seventeen years as his sounding board against slavery. His polished speeches earned him the title "Old Man Eloquent."

In this fight, one thing disappointed him the most. Adams saw in the organized churches the potential to challenge and eventually curb the growing evils of slavery. He lamented the fact that neither the clergymen nor their flocks did much to rid society of this plague. In a pointed letter of May 27, 1838, he wrote:

> The counterfeit character of a very large portion of the Christian ministry of this country is disclosed in the dissensions growing up in all the Protestant churches on the subject of slavery. This question of slavery is convulsing the Congregational churches in Massachusetts; it is deeply agitating the Methodists; it has already completed a schism in the Presbyterian Church.

He spoke his mind; he made enemies. Nevertheless, he was able to maintain respect even from the opposition. Upon hearing of Adams's death in 1843, political rival Martin Van Buren said of him, "He was an honest man, not only incorruptible himself, but an enemy to corruption everywhere."

"The slave has lost a champion," said clergyman Theodore Parker, "America has lost a supporter, and freedom has lost an unfailing friend."

In an appropriate farewell, the Reverend William Lunt based his funeral sermon on the famous passage from Revelation 2:10: "Be thou faithful unto death, and I will give thee a crown of life."

Like father, like son.

ANDREW JACKSON

Andrew Jackson

SEVENTH PRESIDENT, 1829–1837

"First, I bequeath my body to the dust whence it comes, and my soul to God who gave it, hoping for a happy immortality through the atoning merits of our Lord Jesus Christ, the Saviour of the world."
—Preamble of Jackson's last will and testament

His nickname was "Old Hickory," and that wasn't by chance. This gruff military hero spurned the conventional formalities of his day while standing up for principle.

After he had established himself as a successful young attorney in Nashville, Tennessee, Andrew Jackson met and fell in love with Rachel, daughter of Colonel John Donelson. Rachel was in the process of acquiring a divorce; when it became final (or so they thought), the two became husband and wife in August 1791. Due to a technicality, however, Rachel's divorce was not legal; once this technicality was satisfied, two years later, they were remarried.

Nonetheless, Jackson's political enemies, in an attempt to discredit him, delighted in repeating juicy stories about his wife, the bigamist. Mr. Jackson fought numerous duels in defense of her honor, but he could not still the whispers of the Washington gossips. Finally, the strain from the scandal took its toll. Rachel Jackson suffered a heart attack and died, one week before Inauguration Day.

According to biographer Marquis James, the most difficult thing for "Old Hickory" to say was that he had forgiven his enemies. "He made it clear," said James, "that only *his* enemies were absolved. Those who slandered Rachel remained for God to deal with."

Clement Conger, former Curator of the White House, says that President Jackson carried with him a locket containing a miniature portrait of his departed wife. At night, he would open the locket and place it on the table beside his bed so that it was the last thing he saw before falling asleep and the first thing he saw upon awakening in the morning. Today, a painting inspired by that picture in the locket hangs in the lower East Wing of the White House.

Before her untimely death, Rachel Jackson and her husband worshiped together at a Presbyterian church. As a result, several weeks after she died, the President fulfilled a promise to her by uniting with a small Presbyterian congregation located near his Tennessee home, the Hermitage.

But scandal remained a part of President Jackson's career. Shortly after he entered office, he embarked on another crusade, defending a lady with a "tarnished reputation." Young Peggy O'Neal, the daughter of a Washington innkeeper, married Secretary of War Eaton. But because of alleged past indiscretions, she never was accepted by Washington society, especially by the wives of some of the other cabinet members.

Some of the gossip was repeated by the young Reverend John N. Campbell, pastor of the Second Presbyterian Church, which the President attended faithfully while in office. When he heard of Pastor Campbell's contribution to the rumor mill, President Jackson, according to Pulitzer Prize historian Constance McLaughlin Green, summoned the minister to the White House and gave him "a stinging rebuke for maligning a pure and innocent woman." That afternoon, the President severed all his relationships with that congregation.

Beneath his rough edges and hair-trigger temper, the man who once said, "I have only two regrets—that I have not shot Henry Clay or hanged John C. Calhoun," had a deep appreciation for scripture. In his diary, he recorded that it was his custom, in fact, to read three to five chapters from the Bible each day. He wrote to one of his sons-in-law, "Go read the Scriptures, the joyful promises it contains will be a balsam to all your troubles."

Troubles he had, just as did every other occupant of the White House. Yet until his dying day, President Jackson maintained a staunch faith that matched his zeal for living.

On March 24, 1845, a friend, William Yack, recalled that the former President knew death was but a short time away. After taking Holy Communion in the presence of his family, the weakened warrior turned to them and said, "Death has no terror for me. . . . What are my sufferings compared to those of the blessed Savior? I am ready to depart when called."

As his family gathered at his bedside on June 8, 1845, Jackson uttered his farewell. "Do not cry," he said. "Be good children, and we shall all meet in heaven."

MARTIN VAN BUREN

Martin Van Buren

EIGHTH PRESIDENT, 1837–1841

"As to the presidency, the two happiest days of my life were those of my entrance upon the office and my surrender of it."

On Sundays, in Kinderhook, New York, around the turn of the nineteenth century, churchgoers at the town's little Dutch Reformed Church included a small man with striking blond hair whose voice often carried above the rest, especially during the singing of his favorite hymn, "O God, Our Help in Ages Past." This man, Martin Van Buren, along with his family, made public worship a regular weekly habit, even after he became the eighth President of the United States.

President Van Buren's religious teachings and attitudes resulted from a long family tradition. Deeply devoted to the Dutch Reformed Church, he was dismayed at the lack of any representative church in Washington, D.C. As a compromise, he became a regular worshiper—always using a special pew— at St. John's Episcopal Church. On occasion, he attended the New York Avenue Presbyterian Church.

The President knew that religious conviction had its political impact. Early in his career, while promoting the campaign of Andrew Jackson, Van Buren asked, "Does the old gentleman have prayers in his house? If so, mention it modestly."

President Van Buren was nicknamed "the little magician" because he was able to do so much with so little. " 'Tis only by

Interior of St. John's Episcopal Church across Pennsylvania Avenue from the White House. It is known as "the Church of the Presidents." Courtesy St. John's Episcopal Church.

the grace of God," he insisted. His inaugural address struck the same note. "I only look to the gracious protection of the Divine Being whose strengthening support I humbly solicit and to whom I fervently pray to look down upon us all."

The President carried this attitude not only in victory but also in defeat. When he lost his bid for reelection to William Henry Harrison in 1840, Van Buren visited his victorious opponent to wish him God's richest blessings.

In retirement, he spoke out against the evils of slavery and other social ills, but, alas, he had lost his political clout.

In Van Buren's last years, the residents of Kinderhook would wave to their most famous neighbor as he rode a carriage to church each Sunday; when he died, the congregation gathered to pay their respects and to sing, together, "O God, Our Help in Ages Past."

WILLIAM HENRY HARRISON

William Henry Harrison

NINTH PRESIDENT, 1841

"Some folks are silly enough to have formed a plan to make a President out of this Clerk and Clod Hopper."

On November 7, 1811, he won the battle against Tecumseh at the Tippecanoe River. A national hero who was swept into office, first as a senator and later as President, William Henry Harrison is remembered best for his campaign slogan: "Tippecanoe and Tyler Too."

What can be said about a President who served only one month in office? Very little. Yet this is quite possibly more than can be said about the outward signs of religious conviction Harrison displayed.

Tradition records that Harrison was baptized an Episcopalian, although no official record exists to confirm this. While in Washington, he occasionally attended services at St. John's Episcopal Church, across Lafayette Square.

Once, when in Pittsburgh, the then President-elect was seen in his hotel room reading a Bible. The April 13, 1841, edition of the *National Intelligencer* reported Harrison as saying that this was a fixed habit of his for twenty years. "At first," he said, "it was a matter of duty. It has now become a pleasure."

As a result of a long (one hour and forty-five minute) inaugural address on March 4, 1841, a blustery day, the President caught a cold that developed into pneumonia. On

53

April 4, 1841, only one month after his inauguration, the President lay in bed, growing weaker by the moment. He asked that the 103rd Psalm be read to him, showing that he had, at least, some acquaintance with the scriptures. "Bless the Lord, O my soul: and all that is within me, bless his holy name."

A few minutes after the reading of the psalm, the President closed his eyes and died peacefully.

At the Episcopal funeral service in the White House, the Reverend William Hawley, rector of St. John's, stated that the day after his inauguration, the President purchased a Bible and a prayer book. Reverend Hawley held high the two books in view of the mourners and announced that the President never began a day without reading from both. Also, the minister declared, it had been the President's desire to join in full communion with the church on the ensuing Easter Sunday. Neither story, however, is substantiated through any other source.

Was the rector speaking the truth? Perhaps. Yet it would have been sufficient just to say, "Old Tippecanoe has fought his last battle."

JOHN TYLER

John Tyler

TENTH PRESIDENT, 1841–1845

"Nothing but the kind providence of our heavenly Father could have saved me."

—Upon recovering from a serious illness

George Washington was the father of our country, but President John Tyler was the White House father with the most offspring. Our tenth President had two wives and fifteen children. Letitia Christian bore him eight; after Letitia's death, Julia Gardiner (he was fifty-five years old and she was twenty-two at their marriage) bore him seven.

Normally, John Tyler is remembered not for his efforts to increase the nation's population but as the first Vice President to assume the duties of President. As such, he had his struggles with the Constitution. Did the unexpected death of President Harrison mean that John Tyler was the President, or was he only, as the Constitution states, the one who wields the powers of the office?

His political enemies took delight in heaping sarcastic remarks on him for his newly acquired position. "Mr. Tyler, who styles himself the President of the United States" was one of the barbs thrown in his direction by former President John Quincy Adams, for example.

In spite of it all, President Tyler was able to ward off the ridicule mustered by his foes with a calm reserve that matched the biblical admonition from Jesus' Sermon on the Mount, which he learned as a young lad in Charles City

County, Virginia: "Love your enemies. Bless those who persecute you."

Mr. Tyler's life was punctuated by paradox. For instance, in terms of the moral issues surrounding slavery, he was openly a slaveholder who owned a labor force of seventy-five slaves on his twelve-hundred-acre plantation, Sherwood Forest, in Virginia. At the same time, as President, he openly fought for emancipation. He said that the sight of slaves being bought and sold in public made him physically ill.

His life was a contrast even in terms of loyalty to the federal government. When he took the oath of office on April 6, 1841, he swore on an open Bible to "preserve, protect, and defend the Constitution of the United States" and, while in office, took a strong stand against the secession of the South. Yet after leaving the White House, he was elected to the Confederate Congress.

On these, as well as other important issues, John Tyler made enemies in both camps. In describing the slender six-foot President, astute author Charles Dickens wrote, "He looked somewhat worn and anxious, and well he might be, being at war with everybody."

Behind this outward confusion lay a solid Christian conviction. "My life has always been illuminated by a bright faith in the Christian religion," he said. Henry Wise, former Governor of Virginia and close personal friend, remembered the tenth President as "a firm believer in the atonement of the Son of God and in the efficacy of his blood to wash away every stain of mortal sin. He was by faith and heirship a member of the Episcopal Church, and he never doubted divine revelation."

In retrospect, the presidential years were not kind to John Tyler. Outside of the annexation of Texas, no major accomplishment of his can be found in the history books. Since his track record was not sufficient to provide as much as a good campaign slogan, Tyler was rejected by his own party for renomination in 1844.

When he left Washington, it was obvious that his political career had come to an end. John Tyler could never again be elected President, even if all his children had been eligible to vote.

JAMES KNOX POLK

James Knox Polk

ELEVENTH PRESIDENT, 1845–1849

"I prefer to supervise the whole operation of the Government myself rather than entrust the public business to subordinates, and this makes my duties very great."

His middle name, identical to the pioneer of the Presbyterian Church in Scotland, was no accident, for Jane Knox, the mother of President James Knox Polk, was a direct descendant of the famous John Knox. As we might expect, the President's upbringing included daily Bible readings, prayers, and a solid indoctrination in Calvinist traditions. However, a sharp conflict developed between his father, Samuel Polk, and a local Presbyterian minister, the Reverend James Wallis, over a demand for a verbal confession of faith before the service of baptism. Sam Polk stubbornly refused to take such an oath, so young James was never baptized into the Presbyterian fellowship.

One other fact entered the picture. All six children by the second marriage of his grandfather, Ezekiel Polk, were stillborn. Since the Presbyterian dogma of that era included the belief that the souls of unbaptized infants were damned to eternal death, most of the Polk family would have nothing to do with Presbyterianism.

Ironically, in 1824, James Knox Polk married Sarah Childress, a devout Presbyterian who was not without influence, even after her husband was elected President. At the inaugural ball on March 4, 1845, for example, because of the First Lady's strong Presbyterian stance, dancing and the serving of cocktails were halted for the two hours that the Polks were in attendance. This caused Sam Houston of Texas to say that the only thing wrong with President Polk was that he "drank too much water."

But President Polk stood by his convictions, which might explain why he was able to carry out every part of his political program. Since his wife's Calvinist heritage permitted no work on Sunday, he made certain that this applied to the White House as well. Once, when the French minister visited the Executive Mansion on a Sunday, he was greeted by a servant, who told the minister that the President never received guests on the Christian Sabbath.

During his term in office, the President accompanied Sarah to church regularly, but his personal loyalties were with another communion. He wrote in his diary for November 2, 1845, "Mrs. Polk being a member of the Presbyterian Church, I usually attend that church with her, though my opinions and predilections are in favor of the Methodist Church." According-ing to the President, this was the direct result of the preaching of John B. McFerrin. When he was thirty-eight years old, Mr. Polk was deeply affected by the minister's call to a self-awakening. Polk and McFerrin became lifelong friends.

Four months after leaving the Executive Mansion (he was the first President not to seek reelection) and less than a week before his death, James Knox Polk severed his religious ties with the Presbyterians and was baptized and received into the Methodist fellowship by none other than his friend, the Reverend John McFerrin.

ZACHARY TAYLOR

Zachary Taylor

TWELFTH PRESIDENT, 1849–1850

"The idea that I should become President seems to me too visionary to require a serious answer. It has never entered my head, nor is it likely to enter the head of any sane person."

When the stockily built, five-foot-eight-inch, one-hundred-seventy-pounder was an army lieutenant, he was a tobacco-chewing, hard-cussing soul who earned the nickname "Old Rough and Ready." Ready for the White House? Hardly, for he never considered himself as "presidential timber." Ready for the church? Definitely not.

Regarded by most as an Episcopalian, Zachary Taylor joined no church, nor, as far as we know, did he make any public confession of religious belief whatsoever.

In sharp contrast, his wife, Margaret, was a solid Episcopalian who, while with her husband at various military stations during his army career, organized worship services for those unable to attend a regular house of worship in town.

Although President Taylor worshiped at St. John's Episcopal Church, his appearances there may have been solely out of his respect for his wife, who was now a semi-invalid and confined her public appearances to attendance at church.

The only hint we have as to any religious conviction on his part comes from his youngest daughter, Betty Taylor Bliss, who said of her father, "He was a constant reader of the Bible and practiced all its precepts, acknowledging his responsibility to God."

At his unexpected death from an illness rumored to be pneumonia—due to overexposure on a muggy Fourth of July ceremony at the laying of the cornerstone for the Washington Monument in 1850—Zachary Taylor served as President for a term of only 492 days. The public was saddened by the loss of this rugged folk hero.

Praises about military victories and bold leadership echoed from city halls throughout the nation about the fallen President. Few contemporaries, however, found much to say about his accomplishments or, as a matter of fact, about his religious convictions.

MILLARD FILLMORE

Millard Fillmore

THIRTEENTH PRESIDENT, 1850–1853

"Where is the true-hearted American whose cheek does not tingle
with shame to see our highest and most courted foreign missions
filled by men of foreign birth to the exclusion of the native-born?"

—1856

In 1968, just after he was elected as acting President of
Michigan State University, Dr. Walter Adams, employing his
wry wit, predicted that his role as the university's thirteenth
president would parallel that of the nation's thirteenth President, Millard Fillmore. It was Dr. Adams's subtle way of
hinting that his term and contributions at M.S.U. quite
possibly would be forgotten as quickly as those of Mr.
Fillmore.

Outside of being remembered as the second Vice President
to ascend to the office of President due to the death of his
predecessor, Millard Fillmore is recalled as the one who, years
later, escorted President Abraham Lincoln to Sunday worship
services at the Unitarian Church in Buffalo, New York.

When he expressed his religious convictions, he spoke
more of what he was against than what he was for. For
instance, he was a member of the Know-Nothing Party, which
called for the removal of all Roman Catholics from public
office. After losing the election for Governor of New York in
1844, Fillmore blamed his defeat on "abolitionists and foreign
Catholics."

Raised in a Methodist environment in Locke, New York, by
a father who owned only two books, a Bible and a hymnbook,

Fillmore never found it necessary to express his religious convictions in public. Instead, he enjoyed the more quiet contentment offered through the intellectual stance encouraged by the Unitarians.

The President's identification with the Unitarians was short-lived during his brief stay at the White House. After supporting legislation that abolished the slave trade in Washington, D.C., he lent his support to the Fugitive Slave Law, which provided for the return of runaway slaves. As a result of this one decision, the President lost not only his party's nomination for election in 1852 but also his standing in the Unitarian Society, which severely criticized him. Deeply hurt by this rejection, Millard Fillmore left the fellowship and occasionally attended Baptist and Episcopal churches thereafter.

At his funeral in March 1874, a Baptist, an Episcopalian, and a Presbyterian presided. There was no Unitarian.

FRANKLIN PIERCE

Franklin Pierce

FOURTEENTH PRESIDENT, 1853–1857

"Frank, I pity you—indeed I do, from the bottom of my heart."
—*Nathaniel Hawthorne, commenting on
Pierce's excessive drinking*

The poet Robert Browning penned the immortal words:

> God's in his heaven:
> All's right with the world.

Perhaps that's true, but only for those who feel they are on good terms with the Almighty. Franklin Pierce had difficulty believing that he and his Lord were on speaking terms.

Raised in what might be called a classical Puritan tradition, Pierce struggled to reach the level of faithfulness he thought was demanded by the Lord. At Bowdoin College, where he became close friends with classmate Nathaniel Hawthorne, his guilt was increased. Any temptation on his part to relax and enjoy himself was not in character with the strict rules of his college: no drinking or eating in taverns, no attending the theater, no playing cards and gambling, no loud and disorderly singing. In fact, at Bowdoin, any student guilty of "profaning the Sabbath by amusement" was subject to suspension.

Franklin Pierce was never able to shake this yoke of Puritan standards, even after he was elected as our fourteenth President. He maintained the prevailing notion that any personal tragedy was God's punishment for specific sins. Consequently, the deaths of his three sons—the last, Benjamin, just eight weeks before his inauguration—weighed heavily on him and it caused him to write to his law partner:

> I have dwelt upon the truths of Divine revelation and have struggled to think and act in conformity with the precepts and commands of the New Testament—but with indifferent success as every man must who is not a humble and devoted Christian, to which character I can, I regret to say, make no pretension.

His wife, Jane, associated eleven-year-old Benjamin's death in a train wreck with her husband's election to the presidency. She was so affected by this tragedy that she refused to attend Pierce's inauguration on January 6, 1853, when, said the new President toward the end of his lengthy memorized address, "There is no national security but in the nation's humble acknowledged dependence upon God and his overruling providence."

During his four years in office, the President and his wife occasionally attended one or the other of the two Presbyterian churches in the nation's Capital, steadfastly observed a "laborless Sabbath," and took turns leading family prayers. However, none of these acts of devotion was enough to comfort Mrs. Pierce, who was uncomfortable in Washington and seldom attended any social events. Her shyness developed into a deep melancholy over Benjamin's untimely death. She was so distraught that she wore black every day and spent much of her time in her bedroom writing notes to "Bennie," as she affectionately called him.

Despite his Puritan heritage, Mr. Pierce assuaged his grief by frequent capitulation to his love of alcohol, each indulgence resulting in another dose of guilt. Some of his political enemies declared that the President was "the hero of many a well-fought *bottle.*"

After his wife's death in 1863, Mr. Pierce gave up his fight against liquor and resigned himself to the conviction that he would never win his battle for sobriety.

Two years later, he was baptized in St. Paul's Episcopal Church in Concord, New Hampshire, where he could attend services "without hearing a sermon on politics."

For Franklin Pierce, this may have been the only time he was "right with the world."

JAMES BUCHANAN

James Buchanan

FIFTEENTH PRESIDENT, 1857–1861

"There are portions of the Union in which if you emancipate your slaves they will become your masters. Is there any man who would for a moment indulge the horrible idea of abolishing slavery by the massacre of the chivalrous race of men in the South?"

"I have never known any human being for whom I felt a greater reverence," wrote James Buchanan of Dr. John King, the Presbyterian minister of his family's small church in Mercersburg, Pennsylvania, who also served on the board of nearby Dickinson College in Carlisle. Undoubtedly, the accolade was inspired by Dr. King's efforts to have young James reinstated at Dickinson after the spirited student was expelled for arrogance, disorderly conduct, and drinking.

Even Dr. King was not able to comfort the former student several years later, when he was rejected by his fiancée, Ann Caroline Coleman, in part because of her father's suspicion that young James was interested only in her money. (Mr. Coleman was a wealthy manufacturer, while James was born in a log cabin.) In addition, local gossips circulated some unconfirmed rumors about Buchanan and another girl. During the next several months, Ann slipped deeper and deeper into a mental depression and later became mysteriously ill. She died from what physicians called "hysterical convulsions." Embittered members of her family, led by Mr. Coleman, branded Buchanan her murderer.

Overcome by grief, Buchanan wrote a letter to Ann's father requesting permission to view the body and join the mourners at her funeral: "It is now no time for explanation, but the time will come when you will discover that she, as well as I, have been much abused. God forgive the authors of it. I may sustain the shock of her death, but I feel that happiness has fled from me forever."

The letter was returned unopened, and Buchanan was not allowed to attend the funeral.

Close friends of the twenty-eight-year-old lawyer reported that he felt the pangs of guilt for many years thereafter and was convinced that God would never forgive him. Although he enjoyed the company of young ladies, Buchanan never married, making him our only bachelor President.

After his election to the presidency, Mr. Buchanan had other struggles with his personal faith. In his mounting frustration, he wrote to his minister brother, "I desire, so much, to be a Christian," sounding like the man who begged Jesus to heal his son: "Lord, I believe; help thou mine unbelief."

Shortly after entering the White House, Mr. Buchanan had a long heart-to-heart conversation with the Reverend William Paxton, pastor of New York City's First Presbyterian Church. At the end of this meeting, the President announced, "My mind is made up. I hope that I am a Christian. As soon as I retire from office as President, I will unite with the Presbyterian Church." He felt that uniting with a congregation while in office might be construed by his opponents as a political move. He figured he would avoid all this simply by joining a church after leaving the Oval Office.

It didn't turn out to be quite that easy. Mr. Buchanan had endorsed slavery on a limited scale, and he spoke out sharply against emancipation while President. He was refused in his first attempt to gain membership in the northern Presbyterian Church, which advocated abolition. It wasn't until September 1865—nearly four years later—that he was permitted to make public profession of his faith and was invited to join the fellowship in "the church of my fathers," as he himself described it.

On the afternoon before he died, as he lay ill in his mansion, Wheatland, near Lancaster, Pennsylvania, the former President said, "Whatever the result may be, I shall carry to my grave the consciousness that I at least meant well for my country."

That would have made Dr. John King very happy indeed.

ABRAHAM LINCOLN

Abraham Lincoln

SIXTEENTH PRESIDENT, 1861–1865

"If ever there lived a president who, during his term of service, needed all the consolation and the strength that he could draw from the Unseen Power above him, it was President Lincoln—sad, patient, mighty Lincoln, who worked and suffered for the people. . . . If there ever was a man who practically applied what was taught in our churches, it was Abraham Lincoln."

—Theodore Roosevelt, 1903

He was all things to all men. To the slave, he was the Messiah; to the press, he was the Railsplitter; to the North, he was the Preserver of the Union; to the South that knew the Civil War was about to end, he was the Compassionate Victor.

To the Christian, he could well have been Champion of the Faith, except for one thing: Abraham Lincoln never joined a church.

"Nonsense," some say. "President Lincoln was one of our most God-fearing Americans."

But look at the record: Lincoln never *did* join a Christian congregation. Consequently a few scholars are bold enough to ask, "Was Abraham Lincoln a Christian?"

Their question is not new. It was raised even when Honest Abe began his political career in New Salem, Illinois—where he arrived in 1831, as he said, like "a piece of floating driftwood." During his six years there he became friends with Jack Kelso, the village philosopher, who introduced the young Lincoln to the writings of Shakespeare and the teachings of the Bible. Lincoln studied them earnestly, even memorizing long passages. His speeches and private letters often echo the seventeenth-century tone of Shakespeare and the King James Version.

In spite of his familiarity with and love of the Bible, Lincoln still never joined a local church. And his early political opponents used this as an opportunity to brand him an infidel.

Lincoln defended his decision. "I doubt the possibility or propriety of settling the religion of Jesus Christ in the models of manmade creeds and dogmas," he said. "I cannot without mental reservations assent to long and complicated creeds and catechisms."

His answer fell on deaf ears. Meanwhile Lincoln earned a reputation in that tiny community as an outspoken nonbeliever. He certainly did not help his cause any when he openly discussed the writings of Thomas Paine, an agnostic, and enjoyed arguing in private with friends against some church practices.

Because of the sensitivity of his neighbors about the subject, Lincoln avoided the issue whenever possible. "Religion," he said on many occasions, "is a private affair between a man and his God." Later, during his 1846 congressional campaign, he was compelled to meet the issue head on. His opponent—Peter Cartwright, a well-known Methodist circuit rider—openly charged that Lincoln was an atheist and an enemy of the organized church.

"That I am not a member of any Christian church is true," Lincoln confessed, "but I have never denied the truth of the scriptures, and I have never spoken with intentional disrespect of religion in general or of any denomination of Christians in particular."

Lincoln won the election by a landslide, even though his answer didn't satisfy everyone, especially the local clergy.

Abraham Lincoln's most important political victory came fifteen years later when he climbed the steps of the U.S. Capitol, placed his left hand on a Bible, and swore to "faithfully execute the office of President of the United States." He entered the White House with the challenge to direct the course of a nation not yet a century old that was about to go to war with itself.

The poet Goethe may have had someone like Lincoln in mind when he wrote, "God contrives to send during critical moments in history great genius to solve great problems." Part of Lincoln's genius is reflected in his willingness to shun certain things—including an endorsement of one denomination over another—that might further divide the country.

Knowing his religious character, one member of Congress asked Lincoln why he never joined a church. Lincoln replied, "Because I have found difficulty, without mental reservation, in giving my assent to their long and complicated confessions of faith. When any church will inscribe over its altar the Savior's condensed statement of law and gospel: 'Thou shalt love the Lord thy God with all thy heart and with all thy soul and with all thy mind, and love thy neighbor as thyself,' that church will I join with all my heart."

Although he remained unwilling to sign his name on the membership rolls of a particular congregation, Lincoln showed respect for the organized church during some of the more important stages of his career. For instance, he recited his marriage vows on November 4, 1842, to Mary Todd before the Reverend Charles Dresser, an Episcopal priest, and he chose to attend a special service of worship conducted at St. John's Episcopal Church in Washington on the day before his first inauguration.

Lincoln's refusal to join an organized church still gave rise to many doubts about his belief in God. Lincoln himself enjoyed repeating an often-told story about two Quaker women who discussed his potential success as compared to that of Jefferson Davis, president of the Confederate States.

"I think Jefferson will succeed," said one woman.
"Why does thee think so?" asked the other.
"Because Jefferson is a praying man."

"And so is Abraham a praying man."
"Yes, but the Lord will think Abraham is joking."

In spite of the gossip and jokes floating around Washington, Lincoln showed a personal attachment to the Presbyterian Church. He rented a pew, a custom of that era, in Washington's New York Avenue Presbyterian Church (on the right side of the church, eight rows from the pulpit), and he and his family regularly worshiped there on Sunday mornings.

On several occasions the President even attended midweek prayer meetings at this church. But in order not to disturb other worshipers, he often secretly entered through the back door of the building, sat on a settee in the office of the pastor, Dr. Phineas Gurley, and, with the door to the church ajar, listened to the readings from the scriptures and prayed with the people.

One Sunday morning when Confederate forces drew close to the city and the fighting was heavy, Dr. Gurley declared from his pulpit that the next Sunday would be the last in which the church could be used for worship. An order from Secretary of War Stanton had requisitioned the church for use as a hospital for wounded soldiers.

President Lincoln, who was attending worship that day, rose to his feet and said, "Dr. Gurley, we are too much in need of this church these days; we cannot let it be closed. I countermand the order."

Lincoln publicly spoke about this dependence on help from Almighty God not only in church but on other occasions as well. In February 1861, for example, as he was about to leave for Washington to begin his first term as President, he stood on the rear platform of the Great Western Railway train and spoke heart to heart with his close friends and neighbors of Springfield, Illinois.

"I now leave," he said, "not knowing when, or whether ever, I may return, with a task before me greater than that

The New York Avenue Presbyterian Church. Lincoln considered this his favorite house of worship. Courtesy New York Avenue Presbyterian Church.

which rested upon [George] Washington. Without the assistance of that Divine Being who ever attended him I cannot succeed. With that assistance, I cannot fail. Trusting in him . . . let us confidently hope that all will yet be well. To his care commending you, I hope in your prayers you will commend me. I bid you an affectionate farewell."

Lincoln also spoke of his dependence on the guiding hand of God and his faith in the promises of the Bible, especially during moments of anxiety.

Less than a year following the death of his four-year-old son, Eddie, Lincoln learned of the serious illness of his father from his stepbrother John Johnston. Lincoln's letter to his stepbrother reveals the clearest expression we have of his concept of immortality:

> Tell Father to remember to call upon and confide in our great, and good, and merciful Maker, who will not turn away from him in any extremity. He notes the fall of a sparrow and numbers the hairs of our heads; and he will not forget the dying man who puts his trust in him. If it is to be his lot to go now, he will soon have a joyous meeting with many loved ones gone before; and where the rest of us, through the help of God, hope ere long to join them.

On the morning of the funeral of another son, eleven-year-old Willie, a shaken President Lincoln was comforted by the boy's nurse, who assured him that Christians throughout the nation were praying for him.

"I am glad to hear that," replied the President. "I need their prayers. I will try to go to God with my sorrows."

The horrors of the Civil War during the troubled years that followed gnawed away at him. Abraham Lincoln nonetheless kept his courage through private prayer.

A fact well documented in the records of the New York Avenue Presbyterian Church is that before an important battle or at the news of some crisis, whether day or night, the President sent his carriage to bring Pastor Gurley to the White

House. There the two of them spent hours praying for the Lord's guidance.

Lincoln later commented, "I have been driven many times to my knees in prayer by the overwhelming conviction that I had nowhere else to go. My wisdom and all that about me seemed insufficient for the day."

Illinois Senator Lyman Trumbull once complimented the President on his ever-present optimism during the hectic days of the war. "Mr. President," he said, "on Capitol Hill we all wonder that you can do so well in these trying times, especially as you have no precedent to guide you in anything, judicial, civil, or military."

"Please tell the boys on Capitol Hill that I have precedents for everything," replied the President. "Tell them all that I shall commit no dangerous error; that I shall not blunder, because I have precedents, and I carefully follow them. I get my precedents by my bedside at night. I get them while I am on my knees. I seek my precedents then and there; and they come to me from the source of all wisdom."

Kneeling in private prayer was not uncommon for Abraham Lincoln, but his posture was strikingly different at public worship. Normally, Presbyterians of that day sat in their pews for prayer during services. Lincoln, however, stood while praying. His angular, ungainly six-foot-four-inch frame created an awkward contrast while those around him sat with bowed heads.

After one worship service, a curious parishioner got enough courage to ask him about his unusual posture during prayer. Lincoln explained. "When my generals visit the White House, they stand when their commander-in-chief enters the Oval Office. Isn't it proper, then, that I stand for *my* commander-in-chief?"

Lincoln's pragmatic theology helped keep things in perspective. There was the time one devout Christian expressed hope that "the Lord would be on our side." The President responded, "I am not concerned about that, for I know that the Lord is *always* on the side of the *right*. But it is my constant anxiety and prayer that I and the nation should be on the *Lord's* side."

In fact, religion for Abraham Lincoln was always a practical application of biblical truths as the situation called for them. He could be stern when scolding people who shirked their responsibility to earn their daily bread "by the sweat of their brows"; he could be benevolent when he commuted the death sentence of a young soldier who fell asleep while on guard duty. In an era when conservative Christians condemned anyone who attended the theater—"a den of painted women and rogues," they said—Lincoln enjoyed watching plays as a means of escape from pressures of the White House.

Some historians suggest that Lincoln's freeing the slaves was the result of some deep religious or moral conviction. We have no evidence to prove such a claim. Instead his primary concern was the preservation of the Union. He repeated often that if maintaining the practice of slavery would guarantee the unity of the nation, he would endorse it; but he would also free the slaves if that would save the Union.

He hinted at a moral justification in an 1862 message to Congress when he said, "In giving freedom to the slave we assure freedom to the free. . . . The way is plain, peaceful, generous, just—a way, if followed, the world will forever applaud, and God must forever bless."

On January 1, 1863, when he issued the Emancipation Proclamation, Lincoln added, "Upon this act, sincerely believed to be an act of justice, warranted by the Constitution . . . I invoke the considerate judgment of mankind and the gracious favor of Almighty God."

President Lincoln said other things that would please even the most orthodox theologian. On the other hand, he was not above what he called "experimenting" with religion.

In April 1863, probably in order to please his wife, who was interested in such things, Lincoln hosted a spiritual séance in the Red Room of the White House. The medium claimed to reveal secrets "from beyond" through eerie voices that seemed to come from above them. Lincoln treated the whole business lightly, observing that the strange language "sounded very much like the babbling of my cabinet."

Abraham Lincoln is the most quoted of all American Presidents. We are fortunate to have copies of his major speeches and many of his personal letters. Together they paint a portrait of a man who must be labeled one of America's greatest theologians, although not in the classical sense of the word. He neither drafted a system of biblical doctrine nor defended a particular denomination. Yet he was quick to recognize the hand of Almighty God at work in the affairs of nations.

In this regard he sounded like the prophets of the Old Testament, who interpreted events of their day through the eyes of God. Lincoln became a latter-day prophet who saw God as the author of history.

"If the truth must be known, Abraham Lincoln was a fatalist," said his former law partner, William Herndon. Quoting Shakespeare, Lincoln's friend Henry Whitney agreed. "He believed and often said, 'There's a divinity that shapes our ends, rough-hew them how we will.' "

One morning shortly before his death, Lincoln shared with his friend Ward Lamon and his wife, Mary, a dream he had had the night before in which he heard invisible mourners in the White House. He walked into the East Room, where he saw a catafalque with a corpse guarded by soldiers.

"Who's dead in the White House?" he demanded.

"The President," came the reply. "He was killed by an assassin."

Lincoln turned to Lamon and Mary and added, "It seems strange how much there is in the Bible about dreams. There are, I think, some sixteen chapters in the Old Testament and four or five in the New in which dreams are mentioned. If we believe the Bible, we must accept the fact that in the old days God and his angels came to men in their sleep and made themselves known in dreams."

Lincoln may well have been a fatalist, but not in the sense that he believed God did whatever he wanted so all people, both good and evil, suffered the same consequences. Lincoln felt that God's favors were there for those who asked for them.

For example, Lincoln set aside April 30, 1863, as a national day of humiliation and fasting. In his official pronouncement he wrote, "It is the duty of nations, as well of men, to confess their sins and transgressions . . . yet with assured hope that genuine repentance will lead to mercy and pardon, and to recognize the sublime truth announced in the Holy Scriptures and proven by all history that those nations only are blessed whose God is the Lord."

Later that same year, following major victories of the Union army at Vicksburg and other strategic cities, Lincoln revealed more of his personal theology: "No human counsel hath devised nor hath any mortal hand worked out these great things. They are the gracious gifts of the Most High God who, while dealing with us in anger for our sins, hath nevertheless remembered mercy."

On November 19, he repeated the theme in his famous Gettysburg Address, "that this nation, under God, shall have a new birth of freedom."

Lincoln firmly believed that the hand of God would determine the outcome of the Civil War. "The substantial dispute," he said, was between the section that "believes slavery is right and ought to be extended, and the other that believes it is wrong and ought not to be extended." He then added that God's verdict would sooner or later be made evident by "the judgment of this great tribunal, the American people."

Lincoln's creed, like other dimensions of his life, was simple and practical; it was based on the teachings of the Bible coupled with our obligation to seek the help of God. Yet this childlike faith has been butchered by those who attempt to turn the man into something he was not. Consequently, Americans have been robbed of the opportunity to know the rich human side of this man who shaped the future of the Union.

For instance, a few days following the President's death, two respected clergymen of Springfield, Illinois, testified that Lincoln had made a special trip from Washington, where he was baptized at night in the flowing waters of a river. White House records and the President's diary fail to substantiate these claims.

A Roman Catholic priest claimed Lincoln received the sacrament of baptism secretly. No records support this claim either.

Another story from a member of the New York Avenue Presbyterian Church quotes Pastor Gurley as saying that Lincoln had every intention of formally joining the congregation on the Easter Sunday following the end of the Civil War. Again, official records do not confirm this.

Even if this last story were true, we'll never know. As that Easter Sunday dawned, Americans were weeping for their fallen leader who, on Good Friday, had attended Ford's Theater and was torn from the nation by an assassin's bullet.

Was Abraham Lincoln a Christian? For those convinced that Christianity equates itself solely with church membership, the book is closed. For others, his demonstrated faith in the Lord is more than enough evidence to say yes.

Yet there still remain unanswered questions about his faith that enhance the mystery surrounding him—a mystery that can be solved only by Lincoln's own "commander-in-chief."

ANDREW JOHNSON

Andrew Johnson

SEVENTEENTH PRESIDENT, 1865–1869

"Let us stand as equals in the Union, all upon equality. Let peace and union be restored to the land. May God bless this people and God save the Constitution."

—From his last Senate speech

Maybe it was his discovery that some Protestant clergymen actually offered up public prayers for his conviction in the impeachment hearings of 1868 that discouraged Andrew Johnson from identifying with any particular Christian denomination while in Washington.

The man who is best remembered as the man to succeed the slain Abraham Lincoln, and as the only President ever to be impeached, faced an impossible situation. Living in the shadow of a giant like Lincoln, Johnson had extreme difficulty in convincing others that he was carrying out the Great Emancipator's reconstruction program for the battered South. When he declared, "Treason must be made infamous, and traitors must be punished," many linked him with the radicals. Although Johnson was referring only to military and political leaders of the Confederacy, he faced an uphill fight in gaining support.

He did other things to generate political enemies. After President Lincoln's death, some patriotic Northerners thought this poor-white man—the only President who never set foot in a schoolroom—would lash out at the South and punish those who sought to split the Union. Their hopes were dashed when Johnson refused to embrace their philosophy. At the same time, when the nation was beginning to appreciate the ideals of Lincoln, President Johnson sounded an alarm about the potential danger of allowing blacks to vote. "Of all the dangers which our nation has yet encountered," he said, "none are equal to those which must result from success of the current effort to 'Africanize' the southern half of the country."

Eventually this one-man effort to suppress the rights of blacks, coupled with his refusal to join the ranks of those in Congress eager to humiliate the defeated South, led to his impeachment by the House of Representatives. Johnson's removal from office, requiring a two-thirds vote by the Senate, fell one vote short.

What few supporters he gained through this move, he lost when he refused to endorse the Know-Nothing Party's attempts to restrict the liberties of the Roman Catholic Church. Mr. Johnson would not accept, as did some of his forerunners, the concept that "foreign Catholics" in influential government positions were a threat to America's security. To those who believed this, the President posed rhetorical questions: "Who was John Wesley? Who was Martin Luther? Were they alive today, would they be driven back to the countries from which they came?"

While his advocacy of suppression of blacks created enemies for him on one side of the political fence, his closeness with the Roman Catholics was the real slap in the face for those who endorsed the presidential tradition. President Johnson not only tolerated the Roman Catholic Church, he personally endorsed it with his presence at Sunday mass on more than one occasion at St. Patrick's Cathedral, where, as he said, he could "count on Father Maguire not to preach a sermon on politics." In addition, the President publicly praised the Roman Catholic Church for its willingness to treat both rich and poor alike.

It was obvious to his closest friends and advisers that Mr.

Johnson's personal allegiance was to the Roman Catholic communion. Had circumstances been different, he probably would have converted to the Catholic faith. But two things stood in his way.

One, joining the Roman Catholic Church would have been political suicide. Two, his wife, Eliza, a dedicated Methodist who was an invalid for twenty years, would have been crushed had her husband made such a move. Consequently, although his wife was not able to attend church services, the President worshiped at Washington's Methodist churches for her sake.

Deep in his heart, however, Andrew Johnson was a Roman Catholic. Perhaps this was the only church he could attend without fear of some clergyman praying against him.

ULYSSES SIMPSON GRANT

Ulysses Simpson Grant

EIGHTEENTH PRESIDENT, 1869–1877

"Hold fast to the Bible as the sheet anchor of your liberties; write its precepts in your hearts and practice them in your lives."
—*Message in the* Sunday School Times

Frankly speaking, history has given him a raw deal.

Like some others who occupied the White House before and after him, Ulysses Simpson Grant is best remembered for heading an administration racked by scandal. A widespread spoils system employed by successful political candidates resulted in the appointment of less-than-capable cronies to high government positions. Subsequent investigations uncovered a misuse of funds by his Secretary of the Treasury and Secretary of War, among others.

On top of this, the financial panic of September 1873, which forced several important eastern banks to close, gave plenty of ammunition to his enemies, who dumped the blame entirely upon President Grant. But Grant stonewalled with the same spirit that caused his former commander-in-chief, Abraham Lincoln, to confess, "I cannot spare this man; he fights."

"I never forsake a friend," President Grant often said, although many times he probably should have. In standing by his friends, the President became the victim of guilt by association. Nonetheless, even his worst enemies had to admit that Grant was basically an honest individual who suffered from the not-so-honest dealings of those he selected to surround him. History books seldom, if ever, mention this fact.

The same books picture this five-foot-eight-inch, red-bearded, stoop-shouldered President as a semi-intelligent (he graduated near the bottom of his class at West Point), gruff, impersonal man without much compassion. But let's look at the facts.

As Supreme Commander of the Union armies during America's Civil War, he was unmerciful in soundly defeating the Confederate Army and its General, Robert E. Lee. "The art of war is simple enough," said Grant. "Find out where your enemy is. Get at him as soon as you can. Strike at him as hard as you can, and keep moving on."

Northerners proudly called him "Unconditional Surrender Grant." Yet after Lee's surrender at Appomattox Court House in 1865, Grant successfully fought with equal vigor for protection from punishment for Lee and his troops by the U.S. Congress. "The war is over," he said. "We've all had enough bloodshed."

He even made this philosophy a conspicuous point of his 1873 inaugural address. "I do believe that our Great Maker is preparing the world, in his own good time, to become one nation . . . when armies and navies will be no longer required."

Any other acts of charity or hopes for universal peace expressed throughout the remainder of his life were in private. President Grant took little part in Washington's social activities and chose to remain a recluse, sheltered from outside alliances.

As far as the organized church was concerned, he never affiliated with a specific Christian denomination, although he attended several Protestant churches with his wife, Julia. Most frequently the President and Mrs. Grant visited the Metropolitan Methodist Church (now the National Methodist Church), where early records list him, perhaps erroneously, as a trustee.

The most publicized character flaw our history books claim about President Grant is that he was a drunkard. Grant himself encouraged stories about his alcohol problem with such statements as, "I have been convinced that there is no safety from ruin by liquor except by abstaining from it altogether."

While he did fight many battles with the bottle in his early career (once being forced to resign as a captain because of excessive drinking), he never became a slave to alcohol. By the time he reached the White House, he had completely conquered any problem that he might have had in this regard. He even turned over his glass whenever the White House waiters served wine at the dinner table.

The President did, however, smoke twenty cigars a day, a habit disturbing to some fundamentalist Christians of his era, and one which undoubtedly contributed to the throat cancer that took his life when he was sixty-three years old.

A story still making its rounds describes how, when Grant lay on his deathbed, he was subjected to a weak attempt to "Methodize" him. It occurred in July 1885, when Mrs. Grant sent for the Reverend J. P. Newman to pray at her husband's side. As the former President was sinking into a coma, Newman sprinkled water on his brow and uttered the words of the service of baptism, after which he announced that Grant had been "converted and baptized into the Methodist faith." When Grant regained some of his senses and was told what happened, he responded, "Tsk, tsk, you surprise me."

That's the sort of story by which President Grant would have liked to be remembered. But, unfortunately, he didn't write the history books.

RUTHERFORD BIRCHARD HAYES

Rutherford Birchard Hayes

NINETEENTH PRESIDENT, 1877–1881

"I am a Christian according to my conscience, in belief; not, of course, in character and conduct, but in purpose and wish; not, of course, by orthodox standards. But I am content and have a feeling of trust and safety. . . . Let me be pure and wise and kind and true in all things."

—Diary entry, 1893, shortly before his death

"I am a Christian," wrote Rutherford Birchard Hayes, thus making him one of the first men to occupy the White House who, without apparent reservation, publicly pronounced his religious convictions. At the same time, however, although he and his wife, Lucy, attended the Foundry Methodist Church in Washington, the President never became a member. In his diary, he wrote his justification: "I belong to no church. But . . . I try to be a Christian, or rather I want to help to do Christian work." Nevertheless, he did encourage his son, Webb, to attend and to join a church. "While the habit [churchgoing] does not Christianize," he told him, "it generally civilizes."

Visitors to the White House, even today, are told by tour guides the story of how the First Lady, Lucy, proved beneficial to her husband's career. She was an attractive, cultured woman who possessed a conservative Christian character. Her influence alone altered the style of Washington social life. She permitted no card-playing, smoking, or dancing in the White House, and her unwavering stance against liquor meant that no alcohol was served in the Executive Mansion. Her husband's enemies, as well as some friends, called her "Lemonade Lucy."

But the Christian standards of the First Family did not end with mere personal prohibition. There were regular acts of devotion. Every morning, at breakfast, the President and the First Lady held prayer readings, which ended with their kneeling and praying aloud the Lord's Prayer.

Sunday evening hymn sings were not uncommon either, with congressmen, cabinet members, and Vice President Wheeler attending regularly. Included as favorite hymns of President Hayes were "Jesus, Lover of My Soul," "Nearer, My God, to Thee," and "Blest Be the Tie That Binds."

In spite of all this, President Hayes did not enjoy the glories of the office. Part of the reason, of course, was due to the fact that in the election of 1876 Hayes was defeated by Samuel J. Tilden—the Democratic Party's candidate—by more than 250,000 votes. An electoral commission, however, determined that disputed electoral votes in Florida, Oregon, Louisiana, and South Carolina should go to Hayes, thus giving him a 185 to 184 margin over Tilden in the Electoral College. Consequently, President Hayes announced that he would not seek a second term.

When his term ended in 1881, Hayes confessed, "Nobody left the presidency with less regret, less disappointment, fewer heartburnings, or any general content with the result of his term (in his own heart, I mean) than I do." After four years, he and Lucy happily traded the hustle and bustle of Washington for the peaceful tranquillity of home and the opportunity to sit together quietly, sharing a beautiful Ohio sunset . . . sipping lemonade.

JAMES ABRAM GARFIELD

James Abram Garfield

TWENTIETH PRESIDENT, 1881

"My God! What is there about this place that a man should ever want to get into it?"

It had to happen. There came a preacher to the White House.

James Abram Garfield, twentieth President of the United States, was a loyal member and sometimes lay preacher of the Disciples of Christ. "He transports a body to heaven with his very voice," said a listener to one of his sermons.

His messages to churches were akin to those of a traveling tent-meeting evangelist. "I've come tonight to speak with this poor tongue about Jesus," he was often quoted as saying. "I've come to ask you to do what I did when I was eighteen years old, to choose the undying Jesus as your friend and helper, because the hopes of the world are false and the Christian never dies."

After much soul-searching, the call to the political stage drew the young zealot away from the pulpit. Yet the skills of rhetoric practiced in ecclesiastical circles proved a solid base for his ability to persuade in the political arena. At the time of the assassination of President Abraham Lincoln in 1865, for example, the newly elected Congressman Garfield soothed the anger of nearly ten thousand rioters in New York City by shouting, "Fellow citizens! God reigns, and the Government at Washington still lives!"

Even after his election as Chief Executive in 1880, this man who was born in a log cabin—the epitome of the "rags to riches" success story admired by most Americans—maintained a deep devotion to the teachings of the Disciples of Christ, along with his wife, Lucretia. Because he felt that they were contrary to the teachings of his church, Garfield was outspoken in his opposition to both war and slavery. The President echoed the basic teaching of the Disciples of Christ for his strong position: "Where the Bible is silent, there we are silent; where the Bible speaks, there we speak."

We can catch some of the fervent spirit of Garfield's faith when we read his personal testimony as recorded in his diary: "Thanks be to God for his goodness. By the help of God, I'll praise my Maker while I've breath."

As it turned out, that wasn't to be for long. On July 2, 1881, after only four months in office, while waiting to board a train in Washington en route to attend the twenty-fifth reunion of his class at Williams College in Williamstown, Massachusetts, President Garfield was shot by Charles J. Guiteau, a mentally disturbed man who, according to biographer Glenn Kittler, believed that the President had turned into the embodiment of evil and that God "ordered him to kill Garfield."

For three months, the President lay suffering in excruciating pain. A shattered spine, a bullet in the pancreas hidden from the view of the physicians, and a condition too weak to risk surgery, all took their toll. On September 8, 1881, the President heard the pealing of church bells.

"Are they praying for me?" he asked Dr. Edson, the attending physician.

"Yes," Edson replied, "the people of the entire country are praying for you."

"God bless them," said Garfield.

In less than two weeks, he whispered his last words: "I can hear it. I am prepared to die." Within a few hours, the preacher turned President joined the church he had sought all his life—the fellowship of the saints in heaven.

CHESTER ALAN ARTHUR

Chester Alan Arthur

TWENTY-FIRST PRESIDENT, 1881–1885

"I pray God it is a mistake."
—*On learning of the death of President Garfield, 1881*

Two Vermont towns lay claim to being his birthplace. Some historians argue that he was born in Canada. These are but a few of the confusions and contradictions resulting from lack of an authorized biography of the man who served as twenty-first President of the United States. Yet we do know enough to capture some of the personality—the lonely personality—of Chester Arthur.

His father, a rural Baptist minister in Fairfield, Vermont, schooled him in the basic teachings of the Christian faith. However, young Chester chose not to affiliate with the Baptist denomination or with any other branch of the church.

The most influential person, in terms of religious expression, was the beautiful Ellen (Nell) Herndon, a devout Episcopalian who sang in her church choir. When Arthur and Nell began their courtship, many of their first dates were trips to Sunday morning worship services together. After they were married, they continued to attend Episcopal services, although Arthur never identified with a specific congregation.

Perhaps, in time, Chester Arthur would have joined a church and become a staunch supporter of the faith. But even before he was elected Vice President under James Garfield, his beloved Nell died. Friends reported that much of his zest for living seemed to die with her.

On September 20, 1881, at one-thirty in the morning, in his home on Lexington Avenue in New York City, he was whisked into office upon the sudden death of President Garfield. Two days later the still-shocked new President again took the oath of office in the Capitol in Washington, D.C. There he placed his hand on a Bible opened to Psalm 21. He said that it reminded him of the *Te Deum* his wife used to sing in the choir when they attended church on Sunday mornings: "In thee, O Lord, do I put my trust; let me never be ashamed. Deliver me in thy righteousness."

After the swearing-in ceremony, Arthur made a brief emotional statement, which ended with a personal declaration: "I assume the trust imposed on me by the Constitution, relying for aid on Divine guidance and the virtue, patriotism, and intelligence of the American people."

The following years of the presidency for Chester Arthur were lonely. As one reporter said, "Surely no more lonely and pathetic figure was ever seen assuming the powers of government. He had no people behind him, for it was Garfield, not he, who was the people's choice. He was alone. He was bowed down by the weight of fearful responsibility."

Later, Arthur confessed, "Since I came here, I have learned that Chester A. Arthur is one man and the President of the United States is another."

As a widower, he was the subject of rumors about potential romances, and every single woman who attended a White House social function became the source of another story. When the President ordered a fresh bouquet of flowers delivered to the White House each day, the gossip increased. But a persistent reporter discovered that the flowers were set before a portrait of the President's deceased wife, and the gossip ceased.

During his time in office, President Arthur contacted the

pastor of St. John's Episcopal Church and arranged to buy a stained glass window to be placed on the south side of the church. According to the Reverend Peter Larsen, former assistant minister of St. John's, the President, each evening, would sit in the White House, look across Lafayette Square, and see the light of the church shining through it.

The stained glass window donated by Chester A. Arthur in memory of his wife. St. John's Episcopal Church, Washingon, D.C. Photograph by John McCollister.

This may have been the only real source of comfort Chester Arthur had as President.

STEPHEN GROVER CLEVELAND

Stephen Grover Cleveland

TWENTY-SECOND PRESIDENT, 1885–1889
TWENTY-FOURTH PRESIDENT, 1893–1897

"I have always felt that my training as a minister's son has been more valuable to me as a strengthening influence than any other incident in my life."

—1853

An unvarnished résumé would include the following:

Physically unattractive

A former hangman

Father of an illegitimate child

When forty-nine years old, married his twenty-one year old ward

Hardly the credentials for a presidential candidate. Yet Grover Cleveland was elected President, not once but twice, to serve as our nation's twenty-second and twenty-fourth Presidents. He was the only one in history to serve two nonconsecutive terms.

His entire life was surrounded by religion in one way or another. As the son of a Presbyterian minister—he was named Stephen Grover, but dropped the Stephen—he learned the familiar Bible stories very early in life, as well as the accounts of church heroes such as John Calvin and John Knox. Biographer Robert McElroy writes that his early training "inevitably tended to produce a keen sense of personal responsibility, to make trustworthy character. . . . It taught that there is a right which is eternally right, and a wrong which must be forever wrong."

After his father's death, the most influential preacher for the young Cleveland was the legendary Henry Ward Beecher.

After hearing him at Plymouth Church in Brooklyn, New York, Cleveland declared sometime later, "He captured my youthful understanding."

As he ascended the political ladder, Cleveland rose from sheriff of Erie County, New York, where he actually sprang the trap for the execution of two prisoners, to mayor of Buffalo and on to governor of New York, all the while relying upon the simple faith taught to him as a young boy. "Do you know that if Mother were alive," he wrote to his brother, William, a Presbyterian minister, "I should feel so much safer? I have always thought her prayers had so much to do with my success. I shall expect you to help me in that way."

As President, he didn't shed this heritage. At both his inaugurations, he took the oath of office while placing his left hand on a Bible inscribed to *My son, Stephen Grover Cleveland, from his loving Mother.* The Bible was turned open to Psalm 112, which begins, "Praise ye the Lord. Blessed is the man that feareth the Lord, that delighteth greatly in his commandments." In his second inaugural address on March 4, 1893, he expounded on this thought when he concluded, "Above all, I know there is a Supreme Being who rules the affairs of men and whose goodness and mercy have always followed the American people, and I know he will not turn from us now if we humbly and reverently seek his powerful aid."

His fathering an illegitimate child created some zesty talk around those Washington circles noted for gossip, but Cleveland was able to weather the storm of wagging tongues and gave financial support to the child and its mother.

On June 2, 1886, the President married Frances Folsom, his twenty-one-year-old ward. It was the only marriage of a President held in the White House. Officiating at the ceremony was the Reverend Byron Suderland of the National Presbyterian Church, which both the President and his young bride attended. "Uncle Cleve" had been her legal guardian since she was eleven.

Bitter disputes and setbacks in the national economy, marked by the Depression of 1893, made Grover Cleveland's last years in office less than enjoyable. "I am honest and sincere in my desire to do well," he said, "but the question is whether I know enough to accomplish what I desire." After his retirement to Princeton, New Jersey, he received, once again, the admiration of the public.

On June 24, 1908, as he lay dying, he summed up his life and beliefs by his last words: "I have tried so hard to do right."

BENJAMIN HARRISON

Benjamin Harrison

TWENTY-THIRD PRESIDENT, 1889–1893

"It is a great comfort to trust God—even if his providence is unfavorable. Prayer steadies one when he is walking in slippery places—even if things asked for are not given."

—*Letter to his son, Russell*

Theodore Roosevelt called him "a cold-blooded, narrow-minded, prejudiced, obstinate, timid old psalm-singing Indianapolis politician."

While the first few charges are subject to debate, the last accusation is not, for Benjamin Harrison did indeed center his social life in the church—the Presbyterian Church, to be exact. He served as a deacon, an elder, and, at times, a lay preacher. To Harrison, the church was more than a building or an organization; it was a vital dimension of life.

As a child, almost from the day he was born on the farm of his famous grandfather, President William Henry Harrison, in North Bend, Ohio, young Benjamin was immersed in religious instruction—family prayers, hymn singing, and Bible reading. He attended the Presbyterian-founded Miami University in Oxford, Ohio, where he met his future bride, Caroline "Carrie" Scott, the daughter of a Presbyterian minister.

At college, Harrison was torn between two professions: theology and law. He chose the latter, on the conviction that this country needed more Christian lawyers, while at the same time, remaining a staunch supporter of the church.

The Centennial Memorial Publication from the First Presbyterian Church in Indianapolis, Indiana (the church he and his wife attended after he moved there to practice law in 1854), recalls young Harrison's enthusiasm:

> When he came to this place, he lost no time in uniting with the church and taking up such work as he found to do. He became a teacher in the Sabbath school, he was constant in his attendance. . . . his voice was heard in prayer meetings . . . and, whether public or private, he gave testimony for his faith and the lordship of his Master.

His law practice was interrupted by the Civil War. Young Harrison served as an officer with the Union Army and, at the war's end, returned to his law practice a brigadier general with thoughts of running for public office.

"He who wears worthily the honors of the church of Christ cannot fail," wrote his father in a letter of encouragement, "to be the worthy recipient of the honors of this country. Would to God that more of our officeholders were God-fearing men!"

He didn't sound or look much like a politician, but the stout, five-foot-six-inch, bearded patriarchal candidate was elected to the U.S. Senate in 1881. Seven years later, he was the surprise Republican candidate for President.

Even more surprisingly, he won the election—but not the popular vote, for he received nearly 100,000 fewer votes than incumbent Grover Cleveland. Nevertheless, he won the electoral vote 233–168. He was not one who might be deemed "a people's President."

Biographer Glenn Kittler described Harrison as "a cold, aloof man, unapproachable and rather dull . . . a family man, a religious man, a temperate man, and if he did nothing, at least he kept us out of trouble."

On the other side of the coin, the grandson of our ninth President earned a solid reputation for opposing corrupt politicians and the famous "spoils system."

The unexpected death of his wife just two weeks before the election of 1892 left Harrison in shock, unable to complete his campaign. This tragedy, coupled with the fact that he never had gained the confidence of the electorate, contributed to the defeat by his old foe, Grover Cleveland.

After retirement from the hectic Washington scene, Benjamin Harrison returned to private life, serving as an elder of his church in Indianapolis.

WILLIAM McKINLEY

William McKinley

TWENTY-FIFTH PRESIDENT, 1897–1901

"Look after your diet and living, take no intoxicants, indulge in no immoral practices. Keep your life and your speech both clean, and be brave."

—Advice to a young nephew

It was springtime 1853 in Poland, Ohio, a small hamlet a few miles south of Youngstown. Budding flowers displayed signs of new life. Inside the town's Methodist Church, a revivalist talked about another kind of new life. To the front of the church marched a ten-year-old lad who asked to become a probationary member. Forty-three years later, this young man would be elected twenty-fifth President of the United States.

From that spring day until he died, William McKinley kept a close affiliation with the Methodist faith. "My belief," he wrote in 1899, "embraces the Divinity of Christ and a recognition of Christianity as the mightiest factor in the world's civilization." He embraced Christianity, specifically Methodism, with a fervor few could equal.

When he opened his law practice in Canton, Ohio, McKinley joined the First Methodist Episcopal Church and served as its Sunday school superintendent.

McKinley and his wife, Ida, had two children, both of whom died (one was four years old, the other, four months). The shock and grief were too much for the mother and she suffered a breakdown. She never recovered and remained an invalid tormented by epilepsy.

Afraid to leave his wife alone, McKinley cared for all her

needs; when he ran for the presidency in 1896, he refused to tour the country and elected to conduct the campaign from the front porch of his home in Canton. After he defeated William Jennings Bryan and moved to 1600 Pennsylvania Avenue, McKinley continued to maintain his personal care of his wife and broke protocol by insisting that they sit together, even at official functions. His devotion to her remained to his last breath.

While President, he attended Metropolitan Methodist Church in Washington, D.C., and also gathered friends and members of Congress for Sunday-night hymn sings in the White House.

On April 11, 1898, President McKinley declared war with Spain. It turned out to be a 113-day skirmish; as a result, America acquired some Pacific territories, including the Philippines.

When the Filipinos revolted against American rule, McKinley concluded, "There was nothing left for us to do but to take them all, and educate the Filipinos, and uplift and civilize and Christianize them."

On September 6, 1901, less than one year after his election to a second term, the President was standing in a long receiving line at the Pan-American Exposition in Buffalo, New York. The day before, he had received a thunderous ovation for a speech that concluded, "Our earnest prayer is that God will graciously vouchsafe prosperity, happiness, and peace to all our neighbors, and like blessings to all peoples and powers on earth." This day, people pressed forward to meet him in person.

One of the greeters was a young man with a bandaged hand. He was Leon Czolgosz, an anarchist. When the two were less than a foot apart, Czolgosz fired two shots. The President reeled and fell into the arms of a Secret Service agent. As other Secret Service agents subdued Czolgosz, President McKinley lay on the ground. He whispered to reporters, "My wife . . . be careful how you tell her—oh, be careful!"

Eight days later, the President said, "It is useless, gentlemen. I think we ought to have prayer." He then turned to his wife and whispered, "It is God's way. His will, not ours, be done."

President McKinley's last audible sounds before lapsing into a final coma on September 14, 1901, were the words to his favorite hymn often sung on Sundays in the White House: "Nearer, My God, to Thee."

THEODORE ROOSEVELT

Theodore Roosevelt

TWENTY-SIXTH PRESIDENT, 1901–1909

"The religious man who is most useful is not he whose sole care is to save his own soul, but the man whose religion bids him strive to advance decency and clean living and to make the world a better place for his fellows to live in."

"The conservation of natural resources is the fundamental problem."

No, this is not a press release from the Department of Environmental Resources. This timely warning was written by Theodore Roosevelt in 1891 and came out of his Presbyterian and Reformed conviction that the natural resources of the world were given by God to humankind with the admonition to take care of them.

But his religious heritage produced more than lip service. This Rough Rider was another of our Presidents who attended church regularly and stoutly supported the practice, declaring, "I know all the excuses for not going to church. I know that one can worship the Creator and dedicate himself to good living in a grove of trees, or by a running brook, or in one's own house, just as well as in church. But I also know that, as a matter of cold fact, the average man does not thus worship or dedicate himself."

His family was steeped in the Reformed tradition, and young Theodore joined that church when he was sixteen years old. He never wavered from it, which resulted in a minor crisis during his undergraduate days at Harvard. For more than three years, Roosevelt had taught Sunday school at Christ Episcopal

Church near the campus; then the rector discovered Theodore was not an Episcopalian and asked him to join the congregation. "No," said the young man. "I'm Reformed now, and will be when I die." The rector dismissed him instantly.

During his presidency, Roosevelt maintained his support of the Reformed Church. He was so consistently punctual when attending Grace Reformed Church at 15th and G Streets, N.W., that members set their watches on his arrival for the eleven o'clock Sunday worship. One Sunday he was late, causing everything to be upset. After the service, Roosevelt sought out the head usher, D. O. Thomas, and apologized, promising that he would never be late again. He kept his word.

Roosevelt took part in the services with the same infectious enthusiasm that characterized his other activities. He was a particularly vigorous but raspy hymn singer, especially during his favorite hymns, "How Firm a Foundation" and "A Mighty Fortress Is Our God." Worshipers reported that his voice could be heard above the rest of the congregation.

One popular story of the day had Roosevelt reorganizing the heavenly choir after his death with ten thousand sopranos, ten thousand altos, and ten thousand tenors, adding, "I'll sing bass."

He was sensitive to the charge that church people frequently were hypocritical in their everyday lives. At the dedication of Grace Church in 1903, Roosevelt warned, "We must, in our lives, in our efforts, endeavor to further the cause of brotherhood in the human family; and we must do it in such a way that the men anxious to find subject for complaint or derision in the churches . . . may not be able to find it by pointing out any contrast between our profession and our lives."

The tendency of members of one denomination to dispute those of another aroused Roosevelt's ire. "I wish," he said, "I could make every member of a Christian church feel that just insofar as he spends his time in quarreling with other Christians of other churches, he is helping discredit Christianity in the eyes of the world. Avoid as you would the plague those who seek to embroil you in conflict, one Christian sect with another."

Author John Sutherland Bonnell called Teddy Roosevelt's faith a "muscular Christianity," which just about says it all. He projected an uninhibited masculine image throughout his life. At the same time, he disdained dirty jokes and avoided anyone who began telling one. He felt that he had the right to live as his conscience dictated—in an "unpolluted environment."

The President's self-determination led him to reject some of the more orthodox teachings of early twentieth century Christianity, among which was the doctrine of the salvation by faith as promoted by the Lutherans and Presbyterians. "I believe in the gospel of works as put down in the Epistle of James—'Be ye doers of the word, and not hearers only.' " His favorite text, Micah 6:8, reinforced this theme: "He hath shewed thee, O man, what is good; and what doth the Lord require of thee, but to do justly, and to love mercy, and to walk humbly with thy God?"

Self-determined? Definitely! But there were times when his individualism drew a less than enthusiastic response. For example, there was the time he set Washington tongues wagging when he invited a black man, famous educator Booker T. Washington, to dinner at the White House. In spite of the fact that no President before had ever invited a nonwhite to dine at the Executive Mansion, Roosevelt felt that the proclamation "All men are created equal" was more than an ideal written on parchment.

However, there was one event which proved to be a hurdle that even the Rough Rider found difficult to conquer; in fact, it was a political disaster that nearly conquered him. In 1905 the President assigned Augustus Saint-Gaudens, an American sculptor, to design a new penny, along with ten- and twenty-dollar gold pieces. Saint-Gaudens recommended (for purely

The Theodore Roosevelt window

The stained glass window of Theodore Roosevelt as seen at the National Presbyterian Church in Washington, D.C. Notice that even the "teddy bear" is included in the window. Courtesy the National Presbyterian Church.

aesthetic reasons) to eliminate the words "In God we trust," calling the inscription an "inartistic intrusion." The President concurred and ordered the words removed. The new coins were minted and issued in November 1907.

Judging from the avalanche of criticism, one might conclude that the President had vetoed a bill favoring motherhood and apple pie. The *New York Sun* lambasted the coins as examples of "modern barbarism." Representative Morris Sheppard (Democrat, Texas) deplored the "godless coinage." One caustic soul suggested that perhaps the President wished the inscription to read "In Theodore we trust" and to replace the symbol of the eagle with the "teddy bear," named after Roosevelt.

When Congress passed a bill to restore the inscription after July 1, 1908, the President offered no veto, and he no doubt breathed a heavy sigh of relief.

Perhaps publisher Henry R. Luce best put Theodore Roosevelt's individualistic theology in perspective. "My own political hero was Theodore Roosevelt, who, fallible though he was, did not hesitate to assert that righteousness is relevant to politics and all the public affairs of men and nations."

WILLIAM HOWARD TAFT

William Howard Taft

TWENTY-SEVENTH PRESIDENT, 1909–1913

"Politics, when I'm in it, makes me sick."

He did not want to be President, and he sounded like it. He did not want to be a Christian, and he let that be known also.

In stark contrast to his predecessor, William Howard Taft boldly declared a faith that ran counter to the mainstream of early twentieth-century American thinking. "I am a Unitarian. I believe in God. I do *not* believe in the divinity of Christ, and there are other of the postulates of the orthodox creed to which I cannot subscribe."

He was put to the test when, in 1899, he was offered the position of president of Yale, the school he loved so dearly. He refused the appointment on the basis that his convictions were not in harmony with the orthodox Congregational spirit of his alma mater.

While such honesty may be admired now, it served at the time as fodder for his political enemies. "Think of the United States with a President who does not believe that Jesus Christ was the Son of God," exclaimed one critic, "but looks upon our immaculate Savior as a common bastard and low cunning impostor!" However, Mr. Taft was willing to take his chances and threw down the gauntlet. "If the American electorate is so narrow as not to elect a Unitarian, well and good," he said. "I can stand it."

Obviously, Mr. Taft's concern was unwarranted, as this six-foot three-hundred-pound candidate won election to the presidential office by more than one million votes over William Jennings Bryan, the "silver-tongued orator" and outspoken Christian fundamentalist who, years later, would gain further notoriety as the prosecutor and star witness in the famous Monkey Trial of John Scopes in Dayton, Tennessee.

Yet the issue of William Howard Taft's religion still disquieted many Christians. Rumors circulated after the election that, because of his Unitarian views, the President-elect would be unable to swear his oath of office on a Bible—a tradition established by George Washington himself.

On March 4, 1909, because a strong blizzard had dropped four inches of snow on Washington the night before, the inauguration ceremony was moved indoors to the Senate room of the Capitol. The Chaplain of the Senate, the Reverend Everett Hale (author of such stories as "The Man Without a Country"), led the assembled gathering in praying aloud the Lord's Prayer. There is no report available as to whether or not Mr. Taft joined in.

For many of the onlookers, the question yet to be answered was, "Would the President take the oath of office on a Bible?"

The moment of truth at hand. Escorted by Senator Philander Knox, Mr. Taft approached Chief Justice Melville Fuller, who presented him with a Bible. The President-elect extended his left hand and placed it solidly on the leather cover. The crowd murmured and then became silent. The oath was administered, and the new President added, "So help me God." Then he took the Bible in both hands and kissed it.

The few who were able to attend the ceremony burst into a spontaneous applause that lasted for several minutes. In order to accommodate more people, the President moved the rest of the inaugural ceremonies inside the House of Representatives, where he delivered a long address, ending with a plea for "the aid of Almighty God in the discharge of my responsible duties."

The skeptics appeared to be satisfied—at least for the present.

The Washington Star of Monday, March 7, 1909, reported that the President spent his first Sunday in office attending All Souls' Unitarian Church and in relaxation with members of his family. No visitors were allowed; no business was conducted. The Sabbath was declared a day of rest by and for the President.

But Sundays were about the only days of rest for President Taft during the next few years. Splits within the party, coupled with growing criticism of his so-called "infidel" religious views, created tension between the White House and the electorate. And he certainly did not help his cause when he ruffled a few feathers just before the election of 1912. At a time when the majority of citizens viewed the Roman Catholic Church with suspicion, the President said, "I believe the Catholic Church to be one of the bulwarks against socialism and anarchy in this country, and I welcome its presence here."

President Taft's loss of the election of 1912 to Woodrow Wilson may have been due in part to his disregard for political diplomacy. "Taft meant well," said Theodore Roosevelt, who ran against him on a third-party ticket, "but he meant well feebly."

Speaker of the House Joseph Cannon put it more bluntly: "The trouble with Taft is that, if he were Pope, he would think it necessary to appoint a few Protestant cardinals."

In 1921, when President Warren G. Harding selected him as Chief Justice of the Supreme Court, former President Taft was in his glory. "In my present life," he said, "I don't remember I was ever President."

THOMAS WOODROW WILSON

Thomas Woodrow Wilson

TWENTY-EIGHTH PRESIDENT, 1913–1921

"Why has Jesus Christ so far not succeeded in inducing the world to follow his teachings? I am proposing a practical scheme to carry out his aims."

—1919

Can a President be *too* God-centered?

Ask a fundamentalist, and he'll immediately respond, "Certainly not!" A liberal might ponder the question for a while, whereas someone like Sigmund Freud would venture to say, "Definitely." And that's exactly what he *did* say. In his analysis of Woodrow Wilson, the famous psychoanalyst contended that the twenty-eighth President believed himself to be akin to Jesus the Christ.

This man so characterized by Dr. Freud was the son of a Presbyterian minister, often referred to as "my incomparable father." He was schooled in both sacred and secular studies, pursuing the gamut of the academic field from doctoral student in history at Johns Hopkins to a university professorship and the presidency of Princeton University. Through all his academic pursuits, Wilson clung to a solid and uncompromising faith that left no room for debate. "So far as religion is concerned," he said, "argument is adjourned."

Each day of his adult life was accompanied by morning and evening prayers as well as Bible readings. Freud noted that the President "wore out two or three Bibles in the course of his life."

Deeply imbedded in President Wilson's theology was a full

acceptance of the Calvinist teachings on predestination. When, for example, a national or personal tragedy struck, he would argue, "It's only God's will."

Speaking to black leaders in November 1913, he attempted to convince them that their plight was part of God's plan. "Segregation is not humiliating but a benefit, and ought to be so regarded by you gentlemen."

When his wife Ellen suddenly became ill and died in the White House in 1914, the President, believing that such fate was a punishment for sin, sat beside her body for two full days. He stared off into space, speaking to no one, and according to some close friends he came near to a nervous breakdown.

Once in a while, Wilson received comfort from his views on predestination. "I believe in Divine Providence," he confessed. "If I did not, I would go crazy."

Afraid for Wilson's emotional state following the death of his wife, friends of the President arranged for him to meet a beautiful widow, Edith Galt. A whirlwind courtship followed, which led to their marriage in 1915. "She was sent to me by God," said Wilson.

President Wilson won reelection in 1916, campaigning on the slogan, "He kept us out of war!" Ironically, one month after his inauguration, he took America into World War I.

It was during his second term in office that President Wilson was crippled by a stroke and spent the last year and a half in the White House bedridden. According to reliable historical records, Mrs. Wilson handled the affairs of state, leading some to claim that Edith Galt Wilson was, in reality, our nation's first woman President.

The frustration of his illness, plus a series of political setbacks (including the unwillingness of the United States to support the League of Nations, for which he had fought vigorously), turned the President into a defeated man. "You can't fight God," he said quietly.

After he left the White House, the former President, on rare occasions, displayed some of his old fighting spirit. On Armistice Day 1923 he struck a positive chord of predestination: "I cannot refrain from saying it. I am not one of those who have the least anxiety about the triumph of the principles I have stood for. I have seen fools resist Providence before and I have seen their destruction, as will come upon these again—utter destruction and contempt. That we shall prevail is as sure as that God reigns."

For the most part, however, the twenty-eighth President lived his last days in loneliness and bitterness. "I'm just tired of swimming upstream," he was heard to say.

What would Sigmund Freud have said about that?

WARREN GAMALIEL HARDING

Warren Gamaliel Harding

TWENTY-NINTH PRESIDENT, 1921–1923

"If you will talk to God about me every day by name and ask him somehow to give me strength for my great task, I will be thankful beyond words."

—*Asked of a banker friend just before inauguration day, 1921*

In 1921, for the first time in history, American women were allowed to vote in a presidential election. As a result, they helped elect a six-foot white-haired superbly handsome Ohio native, Warren G. Harding, who looked like a matinee idol and carried himself with Washingtonian dignity and nobility.

The first newspaper publisher to be elected to the presidency was not your typical politician. He seemed to be a "Main Streeter" to the American public. He loved poker, golf, and baseball. Instead of barnstorming the country on a whistle-stop tour, Warren Harding conducted a famous "front porch campaign" from his white frame house in Marion, Ohio.

It was this simplistic approach to life that echoed his campaign theme for a return to "normalcy" and swept him into office in 1920 in a landslide election.

Even his personal faith reflected a simple down-home philosophy that appealed to the majority of the electorate. "What doth the Lord require of thee, but to do justly, and to love mercy, and to walk humbly with thy God?" he asked at the close of his 1921 inaugural address, quoting from Micah 6:8, Theodore Roosevelt's favorite text.

Some of his other attributes may not have been as politically advantageous. His physical attractiveness, alone, provoked gossip in vulnerable Washington social circles, leading inside observers to whisper stories about the President's numerous love affairs.

The partners in his alleged extracurricular activities included a close friend's wife—Nan Britton, a beautiful blonde—who reportedly bore his illegitimate daughter. Even famous newspaper editor William Allen White wrote, "What a story! The story of Babylon is a Sunday school story compared with the story of Washington from June 1919 to July 1923."

While all this was going on, the main character in these sordid rumors, Warren G. Harding, countered these attacks with a pronouncement that could have been taken from the book of a traveling evangelist: "It is my conviction," he said, "that the fundamental trouble with the people of the United States is that they have gotten too far away from Almighty God."

The tactic worked. President Harding did not lose public support owing to his indiscretions (real or imagined). Instead, the distinguished-looking Ohioan remained extremely popular. He was indeed a "people's President," who, unlike his predecessor, identified with the average citizen and was never hesitant to call upon the best minds of the day to advise him.

Many biographers attempt to paint a portrait of President Harding as a man with a deep personal faith. However, as they are quick to admit, he rarely showed any outward signs of it. In reality, it appeared as though he considered American business as our ultimate hope. "American business," he claimed, "is not a monster, but an expression of God-given impulse to create, and the savior of our happiness."

The life of this colorful character came to an abrupt end on August 2, 1923.

What exactly caused his unexpected death will probably remain a mystery, for eyewitness reports vary. Some accounts say that the President suffered a sudden heart attack while delivering a speech in Seattle, Washington; many authorities conclude that death resulted a few days later from an advanced case of pneumonia. At the same time, others insisted that he fell from ptomaine poisoning on a train. Some went so far as to speculate that he was poisoned by his wife, Florence (whom the President affectionately called "Duchess"), who feared that the President's lifestyle was about to bring disgrace and possible impeachment. In the eyes of many, her refusal to permit an autopsy supported this theory.

Whatever the cause of the President's death, the news came as a shock. The citizens, especially the women, wept openly.

JOHN CALVIN COOLIDGE

John Calvin Coolidge

THIRTIETH PRESIDENT, 1923–1929

"The higher state to which she [America] seeks the allegiance of all mankind is not human but of Divine origin. She cherishes no purpose save to merit the favor of Almighty God."

—Inaugural address, 1925

William Allen White described him as "a Puritan in Babylon."

It was the time of the Roaring Twenties, when Eliot Ness and the Charleston were household words and people sang "Yankee Doodle Dandy." The stock market was going up while morality was going down, and the Teapot Dome Scandal was rocking Capitol Hill.

Into this den of lions marched President John (better known as Calvin) Coolidge, who gained a reputation as a rigidly moral and an uncompromisingly honest soul who held his tongue and kept to himself. The reporters dubbed him Silent Cal.

"If you don't say anything, you won't be called upon to repeat it," he said.

Some observers felt he was out of place in this society, while others considered him the muted conscience of the nation. Yet no one could argue that his presence in the Executive Mansion wasn't a dramatic change of pace from the flamboyant man he followed.

His presidency began shortly after midnight, in his father's farmhouse in Plymouth, Vermont, on August 3, 1923. Vice President Calvin Coolidge was awakened by the loud banging on the front door of a telegram carrier announcing that

President Harding was dead and that he, the Vice President, should make immediate arrangements to be sworn into office.

Coolidge asked his father, a notary, to prepare for administration of the presidential oath. He went upstairs to dress, but before coming downstairs he fell to his knees in prayer.

Shortly thereafter, in a room lit by a kerosene lamp, he placed his hand on a Bible formerly owned by his deceased mother and took the oath of office from the senior Coolidge, becoming the only President inaugurated by his father.

On the first Sunday after reaching Washington, D.C., President Coolidge and wife, Grace, attended worship services at First Congregational Church. Although they both attended this church as a regular habit, neither chose to become a member.

President Coolidge—laconic, aloof, and a loner—was simple in life and simple in his faith. He felt that preaching should be limited to the standard themes: "salvation by grace," "a change of heart," or "the power of prayer." He became highly suspicious of clergymen who spoke in support of the budding "Social Gospel." "I wouldn't for a minute be critical of the church and its work," he said, "but I think most of the clergy today are preaching socialism."

In the eyes of President Coolidge, the church had a fundamental obligation to our nation. "America," he said in his 1925 inaugural address, "seeks no earthly empire built on blood and force. No ambition, no temptation lures her to thought of foreign dominions. The legions which she sends forth are armed, not with the sword, but with the cross."

If Francis Bacon was correct when he wrote, "No pleasure is comparable to the standing upon the vantage-ground of truth," Calvin Coolidge must have been the happiest man on earth, or at least he tried to be. He loved to seek the truth and pitied those who failed to recognize it. In his autobiography Coolidge wrote, "For a man not to recognize the truth . . . is for him to be at war with his own nature, to commit suicide. That is why 'the wages of sin is death.' "

Although he was known for his reserve, the President did speak forcefully when the occasion called for it.

For a quiet Puritan, that's saying a lot.

HERBERT CLARK HOOVER

Herbert Clark Hoover

THIRTY-FIRST PRESIDENT, 1929–1933

"Bert can take it better than most people, because he has deeply ingrained in him the Quaker feeling that nothing matters if you are 'right with God.'"

—*Lou Hoover, explaining her husband's calm reaction to critics during the Depression*

"I come from Quaker stock. My ancestors were persecuted for their beliefs. Here they sought and found religious freedom. By blood and conviction I stand for religious tolerance both in act and in spirit. The glory of our American ideals is the right of every man to worship God according to the dictates of his own conscience."

These were the words of Herbert Clark Hoover in his acceptance speech for nomination as President of the United States on August 11, 1928. It was a significant statement for the Republican nominee, since the campaign of that year would have religion as one of its primary issues.

Mr. Hoover's Democratic opponent, New York's Governor Alfred Smith, was an Irish Roman Catholic. Many Hoover supporters suggested out loud that a Roman Catholic in the White House would mean the surrender of power by the federal government in Washington to the Pope in Rome. A lot of people accepted this theory. With the aid of this fear in the hearts of American Protestant voters, Herbert Hoover won by a landslide, carrying forty of the forty-eight states. Smith, on the other hand, failed to win even his own state.

But the honeymoon was short-lived. The stock market crash of October 1929 was blamed largely on President

Hoover. Shantytowns that sprang up around the country were dubbed "Hoovervilles," and broken-down automobiles were called "Hoover wagons." Empty pockets turned inside out emphasized "Hoover flags," for to Hooverize meant to economize.

Yet the man who campaigned with the slogan "Two chickens in every pot and a car in every garage" seemed to take it all in stride and refused to knuckle under. When he invited the wife of a Black Congressman to join other congressional wives for tea, he was criticized by the southern press for "defiling the White House." Mr. Hoover countered by inviting the president of Tuskegee Institute and boldly declared that the White House would be "defiled" several times during his administration.

The President, who declared in his inaugural address of March 4, 1929, that "only through the guidance of Almighty Providence can I hope to discharge [the Presidency's] ever-increasing burdens," often attended the meeting house of the Religious Society of Friends in Washington, D.C., where the challenge "I mind the light—dost thou?" is inscribed on a sundial in the garden. Here, like others of his faith, he sought to respond to that challenge and seek assurance from the "inner light" in all dimensions of life.

He needed that assurance, especially when he lost his bid for reelection in 1932 to then Governor of New York Franklin D. Roosevelt, who promised Americans a "new deal." Hoover left office under a very dark cloud.

In the years that followed, at no time did he lash out at the people for their misunderstanding. Instead, he retired in typical Quaker fashion and waited in silence.

His patience was rewarded. Before his death at ninety years of age, he had regained the trust and affection of America. President Harry S Truman (a Democrat), appointed Hoover to chair two national committees and, in 1947, to head the President's Economic Mission to Germany and Austria. Later, in the 1950s and 1960s, he received thunderous ovations from delegates to the Republican national conventions.

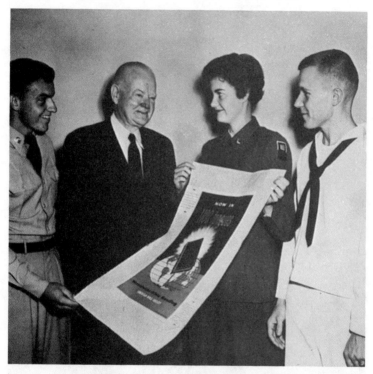

Former President Herbert Hoover, a member of the National Sponsoring Committee of the fourteenth annual Worldwide Bible Reading Observance (held from Thanksgiving to Christmas and sponsored by the American Bible Society), is shown examining a poster depicting the theme for that year: "Now in 1,001 Tongues." Courtesy Religious News Service.

One might rightly conclude that Herbert Hoover lived to see the fruits of patient belief in the "inner light."

FRANKLIN DELANO ROOSEVELT

Franklin Delano Roosevelt

THIRTY-SECOND PRESIDENT, 1933–1945

"I feel that a comprehensive study of the Bible is a liberal education for anyone. Nearly all of the great men of our country have been well versed in the teachings of the Bible."

"I always felt that my husband's religion had something to do with his confidence in himself," wrote Eleanor Roosevelt in her book *This I Remember.* She related how her husband felt that all human beings were given specific tasks to perform here on earth and, with those tasks, the ability to accomplish them.

This was not a high-sounding platitude spoken from an ivory tower. Mrs. Roosevelt drew upon firsthand experience after helping her husband fight the dreaded disease polio, which struck him down on August 9, 1921.

In what would become known as the typical Roosevelt style, the thirty-nine-year-old politician—who had gained national attention in a losing cause as the Democratic Party's vice presidential candidate one year earlier—turned this handicap into an advantage. Astute historian Paul Conkin wrote, "Polio made the aristocrat Roosevelt into an underdog. For him, it replaced the log cabin." Conkin may have been right, for Roosevelt won the election as Governor of New York in 1928.

Four years later, the reward of his patient struggle surfaced as Franklin Delano Roosevelt, offering a promise of a "new deal for the American people," defeated incumbent Herbert

Hoover and became the thirty-second President of the United States by carrying all but six states. It was the first in a series of four consecutive victories—an accomplishment unparalleled by any other President.

Perhaps it was his personal physical struggles, or maybe it was the unstable economy in the country, that led the newly elected President to conclude his first inaugural address on March 4, 1933, with the prayer: "In this dedication of a nation we humbly ask the blessing of God. May he protect each and every one of us. May he guide me in the days to come."

Over the next twelve years, President Roosevelt depended heavily on that guidance. To overcome polio and political opponents at the same time are marks of the inner strength of a determined individual. Perhaps it was this inner strength that urged him on to greater heights. "If you have spent two years in bed trying to wiggle your big toe," he said, "anything else seems easy."

Personal strength notwithstanding, the President was not immune to the encouragement offered through corporate worship. He enjoyed attending church services and became an active leader at St. James Episcopal Church in his home town of Hyde Park, New York. Later, because of his physical limitations, attendance at church had to be limited to special occasions. Nevertheless, during important happenings such as inaugurations, or whenever a crisis loomed on the horizon (especially during the war years), FDR arranged for private services, whereupon he asked the officiating clergyman to seek the strength and guidance of the Lord.

President Roosevelt, whose mellow, resonant voice comforted Americans over radio through his "fireside chats," received his strength and comfort from two sources. The first was the Bible, which he read regularly, his favorite sections being the Twenty-third Psalm, the beatitudes, and the thirteenth chapter of First Corinthians.

The second was prayer. He emphasized this point in the

conclusion of his second inaugural address in 1937. With the threat of war looming over the horizon, President Roosevelt told an anxious nation, "While this duty rests upon me, I shall do my utmost to speak their purpose and to do their will, seeking divine guidance to help each and every one to give light to them that sit in darkness and to guide our feet into the way of peace."

Franklin D. Roosevelt sitting with Francis Cardinal Spellman in a motorcade during the 1940 election campaign. Courtesy Religious News Service.

That divine guidance was never more important than on the "day of infamy," December 7, 1941, when Americans were thrown headlong into World War II by the bombing of Pearl Harbor by the Japanese.

Coupled with his physical ailments, the strains of the years at war took their toll and Roosevelt aged rapidly. During the 1944 campaign, his political opponents used his declining health as a major issue; in spite of this, Roosevelt won an easy victory over the Republican nominee, New York Governor Thomas E. Dewey.

On April 12, 1945, while on a working vacation in the "Little White House" at Warm Springs, Georgia, Franklin Delano Roosevelt died from a cerebral hemorrhage, leaving a weary nation in shock.

Shortly after the President's death, his widow wrote, "He still held the fundamental feeling that religion was an anchor and a source of strength and guidance, so I am sure that he died looking into the future as calmly as he had looked at all the events of his life."

HARRY S TRUMAN

Harry S Truman

THIRTY-THIRD PRESIDENT, 1945–1953

"Boys, if you ever pray, pray for me now."
—*Words spoken to reporters after President Roosevelt's death, 1945*

He said, "Hell." He said, "Damn."

Both got him in trouble, not only with some conservative Democrats and Republicans but also with the Baptist church, of which he was a member. Nevertheless, Harry S Truman was a tough-skinned, full-blooded pragmatist who knew what he wanted and, "if it made good sense," spoke his mind in spite of the consequences.

Harry Truman was not schooled in the sophisticated social graces displayed by his predecessor, and he definitely lacked the familiar "father image" that Americans had so long associated with FDR and others who were elected to the presidency. He refused to play politics for the sake of popular opinion.

"I wonder how far Moses would have gone if he'd taken a poll in Egypt?" he asked. "What would Jesus Christ have preached if he'd taken a poll in Israel? Where would the Reformation had gone if Martin Luther had taken a poll? It isn't polls or public opinion at the moment that counts. It is right and wrong and leadership—men with fortitude, honesty, and a belief in the right that makes epochs in the history of the world."

Harry Truman didn't want the job, but once catapulted into

the Oval Office by President Roosevelt's death, the crusty former haberdasher from the plains of Missouri set out to get things done with a minimum amount of nonsense.

His critics said he was brash; his friends labeled him confident; syndicated columnist Max Lerner compared him to "a bantam cock in a bustling barnyard." By any interpretation, both friend and foe agreed that Truman spoke his mind, in a staccato delivery that was a familiar trademark to reporters at press conferences. And there was no misunderstanding his rancor when he dashed off a stinging letter to the music critic who published an uncomplimentary review of daughter Margaret's singing.

Truman's spontaneous evaluations were aimed at other people as well, including church members. Although, like Gandhi, the President loved his Lord, he sometimes found it difficult to love the Lord's followers. Truman was amazed that those who prayed for "peace on earth" on Sunday seemed to do everything possible to prevent it during the remainder of the week. "The quarrels between religions," he said, "cause many of our world's problems."

When certain groups claimed that "God is on *our* side," Truman countered, "People of *any* race, color, creed, or nation could be God's favorites—so long as they behave themselves."

This is not to say that Harry Truman was opposed to the organized church. To the contrary, the church had been a part of his life since childhood. He met his wife-to-be, Elizabeth "Bess" Wallace, in a Baptist Sunday school in their hometown of Independence, Missouri. Young Harry was only six years old; Bess was five.

President Truman was his own man, of that there can be no doubt. At the same time, he felt that, in the eyes of God, he was no better than anyone else.

He recorded in one of his diary entries that he liked to attend the First Baptist Church in Washington because its minister, the Reverend Edward Hughes Pruden, treated him not as a celebrity but as any other member of the assembled congregation. By contrast, the pastor of another Washington church (unnamed in the diary) turned the occasion of his visits into a "show."

The President seemed quite at home in First Baptist Church and on one occasion gave an impromptu address to the Sunday school children. But this association was soon to change.

In 1952, Mr. Truman was faced with a somewhat sticky situation. A strong ground swell of support emerged in Congress for sending an ambassador to the Vatican in Rome. The President supported the idea and appointed his close friend, General Mark Clark, to the position. Truman knew that such a decision would surely get him in hot water, but by now the President was used to the heat.

However, the Southern Baptist Convention could not stand idly by and let this happen, so at its annual assembly, the delegates chastised its most famous member for encouraging this proposal. Their protests bore a striking resemblance to the warnings of possible Roman Catholic influence in American politics expressed during the Revolutionary period.

When he returned home from the convention, Reverend Pruden met privately with President Truman in the White House behind closed doors for nearly an hour. As he was leaving, some reporters standing at the front gates asked the reason for his visit, to which Pruden replied, "I came to dissuade the President from sending an ambassador to the Vatican."

At breakfast the next morning, the President read an account of this conversation in the newspaper and slammed the paper to the table in disgust, knocking over a half-filled glass of orange juice. "Damn it," he shouted, "this is a violation of confidence!" Harry Truman never again set foot in the First Baptist Church.

In a 1971 interview with Jerry Hess of the Truman Library,

Reverend Pruden gave this account: "I did hear indirectly one or two little humorous remarks that [President Truman] made regarding the situation [appointing an ambassador to the Vatican]. Someone said they saw him at a flower show one Sunday morning, and when he left around ten-thirty, they said, 'Mr. President, are you going to church from here?' He said, 'No, my preacher and I have had a fight.' Then later on, someone said they heard him comment on what a commotion some preachers had made about this Vatican appointment, adding, 'My preacher is the worst of all.' "

When he felt he was right, President Truman was an impossible man to stop. He was in charge, made sure everyone knew it, and wasted little time in "taking matters under advisement." He made bold decisions, whether they involved dropping the first atomic bomb on Japanese soil or firing a five-star general, Douglas MacArthur, for insubordination. He claimed he never lost one night's sleep over any decision once it was made.

Decisions were important to Harry Truman, especially decisions to make something happen for the better. "We often hear it said that spiritual values are indestructible," he once told a friend. "But I think it should be said that they are indestructible only so long as men are ready and willing to take action to preserve them."

His first speech as President to a joint session of Congress contained a preview of coming attractions—a prophetic request mixed with religious overtones—"that I may discern between good and bad; for who is able to judge . . . so great a people? I only ask to be a good and faithful servant of my Lord and my people."

That rather lofty-sounding ideal notwithstanding, he repeated this thought in a manner that reflected more the Truman style when he told his daughter, Margaret, "Your dad will never be reckoned among the great. But you can be sure he did his level best and gave all he had to his country. There is an epitaph in Boot Hill Cemetery in Tombstone, Arizona, which reads, 'Here lies Jack Williams; he done his damnedest.' What more can a person do?"

That was classic Harry Truman. His quest to do the best with what the good Lord gave him underlined his entire life. The following note, in his own handwriting, was attached to Harry Truman's favorite prayer that he kept on his White House desk. The President also carried a copy of it with him at all times.

This prayer has been said by me—Harry S Truman—from high school days, as a window washer, bottle duster, floor scrubber in an Independence, Missouri, drugstore, as a time-keeper on a railroad contract gang, as an employee of a newspaper, as a bank clerk, as a farmer riding a gangplow behind four horses and mules, as a fraternity official learning to say nothing at all if good could not be said of a man, as a public official judging the weaknesses and shortcomings of constituents, and as President of the United States of America.

> *O, almighty and everlasting God,*
> *creator of heaven and earth and the universe:*
> *Help me to be, to think, to act what*
> *is right, because it is right.*
> *Make me truthful, honest, and honorable*
> *in all things.*
> *Make me intellectually honest for the*
> *sake of right and honor, and without thought*
> *of reward to me.*
> *Give me the ability to be charitable,*
> *forgiving, and patient with my fellow men.*
> *Help me to understand their motives and*
> *their shortcomings—even as Thou understandest*
> *mine.*
> *Amen.*

President Truman was a pragmatist, not only in politics but in theology as well. "The Sermon on the Mount," he said, "is the greatest of all things in the Bible, a way of life, and maybe someday men will get to understand it as the *real* way of life."

To Harry Truman, that made good sense.

DWIGHT DAVID EISENHOWER

Dwight David Eisenhower

THIRTY-FOURTH PRESIDENT, 1953–1961

"Every gun that is made, every warship launched, every rocket fired signifies, in the final sense, a theft from those who hunger and are not fed, those who are cold and are not clothed. This world in arms is not spending money alone. It is spending the sweat of its laborers, the genius of its scientists, the hopes of its children. . . . This is not a way of life at all, in any true sense. Under the cloud of threatening war, it is humanity hanging from a cross of iron."

"If there was nothing else in my life to prove the existence of an almighty and merciful God, the events of the next twenty-four hours did it. This is what I found out about religion: It gives you courage to make the decisions you must make in a crisis, and then the confidence to leave the results to a higher power. Only by trust in oneself and trust in God can a man carrying responsibility find repose."

With these words, General Dwight David Eisenhower recalled his anxiety over the postponement of D-Day in June 1944. He maintained this personal theology when he served as the thirty-fourth President of the United States.

Before his inauguration in 1953, the former Supreme Commander of the Allied armies in Europe during World War II, elected President in a sweeping victory over Democratic rival Adlai Stevenson, composed a prayer. It read, in part:

Almighty God, as we stand here at this moment, my future associates in the executive branch of government join me in beseeching that thou will make full and complete our dedication to the service of the people in this throng, and their fellow citizens everywhere.

Give us, we pray, the power to discern right from wrong, and allow all our words and actions to be governed thereby, and by the laws of our land.

With this prayer, on January 20, 1953, Eisenhower began his inaugural address. While most other Presidents refer to Almighty God at the conclusion of their first official speeches to the American public—as if this were an appropriate way to sign off—Dwight Eisenhower was the only one who boldly began his inaugural address with a prayer.

Prayer had always been a part of Dwight Eisenhower's Christian heritage. At the same time, some of the other so-called "normal" activities associated with the faith were missing.

The Eisenhower family in Abilene, Kansas, belonged to the River Brethren sect, which frowned on infant baptism. Hence, young Ike just never got around to being baptized.

Not until after much prayerful consideration, on February 1, 1953, less than two weeks following his inauguration, did President Eisenhower kneel before the font at the National Presbyterian Church for the rite of Holy Baptism. "He has moved from one army post to another and has never staked down his faith," said the officiating clergyman, Dr. Edward L. R. Elson, immediately following the private ceremony in the church.

During his administration, the President began several traditions that had a religious emphasis, including a practice of beginning each meeting of the Cabinet with a silent prayer and also hosting the first presidential prayer breakfast at Washington's Mayflower Hotel. The tradition became so popular that overflow crowds dictated moving the breakfast to the more spacious Hilton Hotel, where the breakfasts are held to this day.

On Sunday mornings, the President would be seen entering the National Presbyterian Church. When on several occasions the President returned to the White House from an extended trip abroad, and it happened to be on a Sunday morning, he would step from the helicopter, speak a few words to the press, go inside to change clothes, and immediately head for church services.

However, as all Presidents are quick to realize, there was little he could do without becoming subjected to criticism. President Eisenhower's practice of attending church drew comments from Senator Matthew Neeley (Democrat, West Virginia) who charged that the President's public worship smacked of hypocrisy. He felt that if the President wanted to pray, he should "shut the door and pray in secret."

Upon leaving the White House after two four-year terms, the former President and his wife, Mamie, became members of the Presbyterian Church of Gettysburg, Pennsylvania, on February 1, 1961 (the anniversary of his baptism). His new pastor, the Reverend Robert A. MacAskill, recalls, "The Eisenhowers set a good example by their regular attendance at worship, and they made the rest of us feel better just by being there."

Pastor MacAskill points to the fact that President Eisenhower endorsed a strong concept of "a sovereign God who ruled all nations and peoples."

The pastor, who was undoubtedly closer to this President than was any other clergyman, summarized Eisenhower's basic approach to his faith: "If each of us in his own mind would dwell upon the simple virtues—integrity, courage, self-confidence, and unshakable belief in his Bible—would not some of our problems tend to simplify themselves?"

Straightforward and to the point: That was Dwight David Eisenhower.

JOHN FITZGERALD KENNEDY

John Fitzgerald Kennedy

THIRTY-FIFTH PRESIDENT, 1961–1963

"I am not the Catholic candidate for President. I am the Democratic Party's candidate for President who happens to be a Catholic."
—*Campaign speech, 1960*

He had all the credentials of a superb presidential candidate. He came from a solid New England family. He was wealthy, handsome, articulate, brilliant, energetic, and clever. Only one thing stood in his way. He was a Roman Catholic.

During the early days of the campaign of 1960, John Fitzgerald Kennedy's Roman Catholic faith caused even some of the staunchest Democrats to fear that, if elected, his policies (and those of the nation) would be dictated by the Vatican. Others feared that his Catholic heritage would hurt any chance of gaining election as it did for candidate Alfred E. Smith in 1928.

Pockets of fundamentalism coupled with anti-Catholic prejudice still existed in the nation, particularly in the so-called Bible Belt states—North and South Carolina, Tennessee, Kentucky, Georgia, Florida, Mississippi, Alabama, Arkansas, and Texas. Many Protestants feared that, were Kennedy elected as President, our national policies would be shaped not in Washington but in Rome. They were concerned that as President, Kennedy would be compelled to follow the dictates of the Pope.

In typical style, the young Massachusetts Democrat met the issue head on, leaving no doubt as to where he stood on the subject of church and state—particularly as it related to the presidency. Just eight months before the election in 1960, Kennedy spelled out his philosophy in a *Look* magazine article. "Whatever one's religion in his private life may be," he wrote, "for the office-holder nothing takes precedence over his oath to uphold the Constitution and all of its parts— including the First Amendment and the strict separation of church and state."

One month later he told a group of newspaper editors, "I am not the Catholic candidate for President. I do not speak for the Catholic Church on issues of public policy, and no one in that church speaks for me."

Perhaps he was most convincing when he gave a dramatic speech in September before a gathering of Protestant ministers in Houston, Texas. Here he displayed the famous Kennedy ability to turn adversity into advantage when he told them, "Because I am a Catholic, and no Catholic has been elected President, it is apparently necessary for me to state once again . . . not what kind of church I believe in, for that should be important only to me, but what kind of America I believe in. I believe in an America where separation of church and state is absolute, where no Catholic prelate would tell the President (should he be Catholic) how to act, and no Protestant minister would tell his parishioners for whom to vote."

Aside from his remarkable ability to win over even his strongest critics, Kennedy had three other advantages over former Catholic candidate Al Smith. First, the spirit of peaceful coexistence perpetuated by President Eisenhower did much to ease tensions between Roman Catholics and Protestants. Second, the Catholic Church made a conscientious effort to downplay its familiar claim as being the "only true church." Finally, the presence of Pope John XXIII in the Vatican was of great comfort to both Catholics and non-Catholics. This fatherly figure who radiated love and concern for all God's children quickly dispelled any notion that Rome was a threat to the security of the United States. John XXIII was a new breed of pope; John Kennedy represented the modern version of Catholicism.

John Kennedy won the election in 1960, but it was not easy. He squeezed past the Republican nominee, Richard Nixon, by less than 113,000 votes. Some analysts felt that Kennedy's religion helped him as much as it hurt him in the election. Nevertheless, it was the President's conduct that did the most to keep the matter stilled during his 1,036 days in office.

Although he was a faithful attender of mass, the President was reluctant to invite Roman Catholic priests to the Executive Mansion for fear of misinterpretation by the press and other observers. Also, during his administration, he showed no religious favoritism in his selection of staff members; he recommended no ambassador to the Vatican (something which even Harry Truman, a Baptist, had considered); he did not hinder legislation regarding birth control; and, on occasion, he attended special services at Protestant churches.

As was the case with most Chief Executives, President Kennedy remained cautious about confiding in others, even to clergymen; while he was President, he often worried that a visit to the confession booth (a standard procedure for faithful Catholics) would prove disastrous were some priest to recognize his voice and reveal the contents of his confession. In order to avoid recognition as much as possible, the President attended confession along with a group of Roman Catholic Secret Service agents and waited his turn in line with other parishioners.

In the popular compendium *The People's Almanac*, Michael Medved relates that once, when the President entered the booth, his familiar voice was recognized by the priest.

"Good evening, Mr. President," said the priest.

"Good evening, Father," answered Kennedy, who then quickly arose and walked out.

In spite of this, President Kennedy counted among his

friends two priests in whom he placed his trust. One was Richard Cardinal Cushing of Boston. An old friend of the Kennedy clan, he officiated at Kennedy's marriage to socially prominent Jacqueline Bouvier in 1953 and baptized their children.

The other confidant was his "pastor in Washington"—Father Albert Pereira of St. Stephen's Church in Middleburg, Virginia, near a country home purchased by the President and Mrs. Kennedy in 1961. The President would often arrive a few minutes before mass in order to chat privately with Father Pereira and, according to the priest, displayed a remarkable awareness of the finer points of Catholic dogma.

Former U.S. Senate Chaplain Edward Elson agrees with Father Pereira. "President Kennedy found it easy to talk about his religious convictions," he told this reporter. "At the same time, he was highly aware of the necessity to keep religion and matters of state separate."

John Kennedy had an uncanny ability to sway crowds. His youth, charm, and polish created a vibrant charisma, not only in America but in other lands as well.

In 1961, during a visit to France at a time when fashion-minded designers copied his wife's stylish clothes and hair-dos, the President introduced himself as "the man who accompanied Jacqueline Kennedy to Paris."

Later that year, he stood alongside the Berlin Wall, which separated family and friends of West Germany and East Germany. He captured the hearts of the people, drawing cheers from an assembled throng, as he proclaimed his empathy by shouting, *"Ich bin ein Berliner!"*

Perhaps his personal ethos was never more evident than at the time he returned to the soil of his ancestors in the spring of 1963 and spoke to the people of Ireland about his heritage: "When my great-grandfather left here, he carried with him two things—a strong religious faith and a strong desire for

President Kennedy with Pope Paul VI at Vatican City. Kennedy, the first Catholic chief executive, was the third U.S. President to visit a Pope during his term in office. Courtesy Religious News Service.

liberty. I am glad to say that all of his great-grandchildren valued that inheritance."

On Friday, November 22, of that same year, a weeping world had at least this legacy for which to be thankful. At 12:30 P.M. in Dallas, Texas, a sniper's bullet killed the President of the United States.

LYNDON BAINES JOHNSON

Lyndon Baines Johnson

THIRTY-SIXTH PRESIDENT, 1963–1969

"No man could live in the house where I live and work at the desk where I work, without needing and seeking the support of earnest and frequent prayer. Prayer has helped me bear the burdens of the first office, which are too great to be borne by anyone alone."

Lyndon Baines Johnson was a crowd pleaser. Nothing delighted him more than to win the admiration of the multitudes. To the dismay of Secret Service agents, the President often slipped out of their protective ring just to shake hands with people along a parade route or, without warning, took a break from the routine of the Oval Office and walked outside to talk with visitors standing in line awaiting a tour of the White House. Why? Lyndon Johnson simply loved their attention and behaved much like an actor who lives on applause.

Because he wanted to please everybody, it came as no surprise that the thirty-sixth President attended more Washington churches—both Protestant and Catholic—than any other President. Even on the day of his inauguration in 1965, he played both sides of the ecumenical fence. At nine o'clock in the morning, with Vice President Hubert H. Humphrey and other national leaders, President Johnson attended an interfaith religious service—the first of its kind for a President—at the National City Christian Church, at which a Catholic priest, a Protestant minister, and a rabbi offered prayers.

Attending church service was not always a retreat from his problems, for on November 12, 1967, while worshiping at historic Bruton Parish Church in Williamsburg, Virginia, the

President was chastised from the pulpit for his policies on Vietnam. Upon leaving the service, his wife, Lady Bird, fuming inside but keeping her composure, let it be known to the Reverend Cotesworth Pinckney Lewis how she felt about his sermon. "The choir anthem was lovely," she said.

For reasons known only to himself, President Johnson surrounded himself with advisers who had strong church ties, such as Press Secretary Bill Moyers, an ordained Baptist minister, and evangelist Billy Graham, a frequent visitor to the White House, who was labeled by the press as a "member of the Cabinet, ex officio."

President Johnson worked hard, played hard, and prayed hard. "No man could live in the house where I live," he said, "and work at the desk where I work, without needing and seeking the support of earnest and frequent prayer. Prayer has helped me to bear the burdens of the first office, which are too great to be borne by anyone alone."

The burdens to which he referred were suddenly thrust upon him by the sniper's bullet that killed President John F. Kennedy on the afternoon of November 22, 1963. The entire world ground to a halt and watched as the tragic events unfolded, including a video replay of the shooting . . . a rush of cars to the hospital . . . a blood-stained pink suit . . . a bronze coffin . . . and a tall Texan aboard Air Force One with his left hand on President Kennedy's personal Bible, haltingly raising his right hand to take the oath of office from Justice Sarah Hughes. Lyndon Baines Johnson became the President of a nation in mourning.

At one minute before six, Washington time, Air Force One landed at Andrews Air Force Base. It was dark. Only after the body of the fallen President, accompanied by Mrs. Kennedy, was removed from the plane did the newly sworn President appear. He was drawn, tired, disheveled, and bent over like a man twice his age. He approached a microphone, reached into

Lyndon B. Johnson taking the oath of office aboard Air Force One shortly after the assassination of President Kennedy. Mrs. Kennedy is seen standing in foreground with Mrs. Johnson to the right of President Johnson. Courtesy Religious News Service.

his coat pocket, drew out a piece of paper, and delivered the shortest inaugural address in the nation's history.

"This is a sad time for all people. We have suffered a great loss that cannot be weighed.

'For me, it is a deep personal tragedy. I know the world shares the sorrow that Mrs. Kennedy and her family bear.

"I will do my best. That is all I can do. I ask for your help—and God's."

But Lyndon Johnson did not like funerals, and he was not going to let the effects of this one linger any longer than necessary. He was a man who enjoyed getting things done. With his political savvy, he played Congress like a master musician would his violin. He had relentless drive, and if fighting and arm twisting were necessary, so be it.

One of the driving forces behind the new President was his obsession with a dream for a better America—a compassionate, loving, and caring America. He fought for what he called the Great Society, where everyone—rich or poor, black or white—could prosper.

Lyndon Johnson treated this compelling drive to serve humanity like a mandate from God. At a presidential prayer breakfast on February 1, 1961, then Vice President Johnson had said, "We need to remember that the separation of church and state must never mean the separation of religious values from the lives of public servants. If we who serve free men today are to differ from the tyrants of this age, we must balance the powers in our hands with God in our hearts."

Later that same year, at a Christmas pageant for peace, Johnson boldly proclaimed, "Let no one mistake the American purpose. Our nation is dedicated to Christ's quest for peace—not the false peace of evasion and retreat, but the divine peace which comes as the fulfillment of striving and the climax of commitment. We shall never falter in that dedication."

These were not his goals alone; the President insisted that the author of such a society was Almighty God, and he once suggested that a monument be built in the capital, a city full of monuments, in God's honor. This idea never got beyond the planning stage, and to the astonishment of the President it was the conservative church leaders who rebelled. In their opinion, such a monument might imply support of the claim by radical theologians that "God is dead."

Lyndon B. Johnson shook his head in utter disbelief. This interpretation was impossible for someone who was such a great believer in himself, in his nation, and in his God.

RICHARD MILHOUS NIXON

Richard Milhous Nixon

THIRTY-SEVENTH PRESIDENT, 1969–1974

"Mr. Nixon would have profited by a pastor. Billy Graham, who frequented the White House, is an evangelist; this is a different breed from a pastor. Every man in this world has the right to have a spiritual confidant to whom he can say anything and from whom he can hear anything."

—*Dr. Edward L. R. Elson, former U.S. Senate chaplain, 1978*

"When the history books are written," said an Associated Press release of August 9, 1974 (the day Nixon resigned from office), "the Presidency of Richard Milhous Nixon will be placed in its proper perspective."

Most people find it difficult to be objective about him. Visitors to Tussaud's Wax Museum in London answered questionnaires which asked, "What person do you most hate and fear?" Topping the list in 1974 was Richard Nixon. Today, some observers—in America and throughout the world— regard him as a martyr and even a folk hero.

Both the man and his political career were marked with personal triumphs and rocked by bitter defeats. Friends he trusted betrayed him and confidential communications were leaked to the press. Stories were blown out of proportion.

The former Vice President under Dwight Eisenhower lost the presidential election of 1960 and the race for governor of California in 1962. The defeats hurt him deeply—especially the one in '62, after which Nixon vowed never again to enter the arena of politics. Yet after a time for healing, he again thrust himself into the spotlight and pushed forward against incredible odds. He regained his national popularity and won the election for President in 1968 by a plurality; in 1972, he won reelection by the largest majority of any presidential candidate in history until that time.

Because of his unwavering self-determination and inner conviction, it is difficult to pigeonhole Richard Nixon in terms of his principles—including his religious beliefs. When he was nine years old, his parents moved to Whittier, California, then a small Quaker community, and that is the closest connection the thirty-seventh President had with the Religious Society of Friends. His youth, he said, consisted of "family, church, and school." But as he grew older, he parted ways with his fellow Quakers.

Unlike Herbert Hoover (the only other Quaker President), Mr. Nixon never attended the Friends meeting house in Washington, D.C. Instead, he seemed quite comfortable with a variety of other communions, choosing to attend different churches without identifying with any one of them.

The now famous tapes of White House conversations in the Oval Office during the Nixon administration (made public during the Watergate hearings) revealed that the President's actions were guided by a passion for maintaining the sovereignty of his office coupled with bitter memories of those former confidants who he felt had betrayed him. This could explain why Mr. Nixon kept himself at arm's length from both individuals and organizations and perhaps why he became so "religiously insulated" against the organized church.

The spiritual adviser closest to the President was evangelist Billy Graham. According to former speech writer Pat Buchanan, the entire White House staff once went en masse to a Billy Graham crusade in Pittsburgh. "It was the President's idea," said Buchanan.

Billy Graham was a favorite of President Nixon. According to Dr. Edward Elson, former chaplain of the U.S. Senate, "Mr. Nixon would have profited by a pastor. Billy Graham . . . is an evangelist; this is a different breed from a pastor. Every man in this world has the right to have a spiritual confidant to whom he can say anything and from whom he can hear anything."

Chaplain Elson's comments invite debate; nonetheless, Mr. Nixon's association with Billy Graham may have been one of the reasons why the President shunned public worship. After just sixteen months in office, the President appeared as a guest at one of the Graham crusades. But as he attempted to speak from the platform, Mr. Nixon was heckled by antiwar protesters in the audience.

The President's closest association with a church and its congregational life was in Key Biscayne, Florida, where he spent many days during his administration relaxing and enjoying life with his friend Bebe Rebozo. The Reverend John Huffman, pastor of Key Biscayne Presbyterian Church, tells how the President was a frequent visitor to services. On the day the Vietnam War finally ended, the President requested a special service of prayer to be held at the church that evening.

Outside of that, Mr. Nixon seldom attended public worship. Instead, he devised a new plan. Shortly after his inauguration in 1969, he invited prominent clergymen throughout the country to come to the Executive Mansion on Sunday mornings to lead an assembled body of three hundred to four hundred people—also invited by the President—in worship in the East Room. Arrangements were made through Bud Wilkerson, former Oklahoma University football coach, who carefully outlined the protocol for the invited clergymen, which included the admonition to limit the sermon to fifteen minutes, because "the President doesn't like long messages."

This unique arrangement often proved frustrating to the designated minister. Owing to the President's erratic schedule, sometimes the call went out as late as Friday to a minister, who was asked to rearrange his schedule, pack his suitcase, and be in Washington before ten o'clock on Sunday morning.

If this mode of worship didn't shatter precedent, it bent it out of recognizable shape. Like the rest of us mortals, even a Chief Executive who attempts to alter tradition is vulnerable to public rebuke, and in a June 1969 edition of the *Washington Daily News* President Nixon's style of worship was criticized as a "Madison Avenue gimmick."

"Who does he think he is? Why doesn't he attend church like everyone else?" some asked.

Reinhold Niebuhr, prominent American theologian, was even stronger in his criticism. "President Nixon has turned the East Room into a kind of sanctuary and, by a curious combination of innocence and guile, has circumvented the Bill of Rights' first article."

The President explained his intramural approach to worship this way: "I could not as President attend a regular church service without being a source of distraction to the congregation and the cause of all manner of special preparation." However, his explanation fell upon deaf ears, and after two short years this practice quietly faded away.

One psychologist was reported in a national news story to have remarked that President Nixon's "chapel in the White House" approach to worship was akin to the lifestyle of a European king who lived in a castle with its own chapel. "It shows that this man really sought to be a king rather than a president," said the psychologist. That remark brought back memories of the time the President attempted to dress White House guards in white military uniforms fashioned by a European designer. This, too, resembled the trappings of monarchy.

These reactions were only foretastes of the future. As so often happened during his term of office, when President Nixon attempted to do what he thought was right, he suffered a setback in the eyes of many Americans.

Setbacks were certainly nothing new to this President. Moving to New York to practice law following his defeat for the governorship of California in '62, Nixon was a forgotten man. Most considered him a political lightweight. Even those close to him kept him at arm's length: everyone, that is, except one—fellow attorney John Mitchell. Their friendship had deepened in those lonely years during which Nixon inched his way back up the political ladder. After what the Associated Press labeled the "greatest comeback of all time" in the presidential victory of 1968, Nixon appointed his dear friend John Mitchell as Attorney General.

On June 17, 1972, five men were apprehended while burglarizing the Democratic National Committee's headquarters in the Watergate Building. John Mitchell told the President that he—Mitchell—was involved. The President, out of loyalty, tried to protect his trusted friend through a cover-up that failed miserably. Taped conversations, congressional investigations, sworn testimony by eyewitnesses, and public outcries sealed his fate.

The Oval Office of the White House is said to be the loneliest room in the world. When occupied by a rugged individualist so dedicated to the protection of this office, its demands eventually were bound to bring the President to his knees, especially in the wake of such a major trauma.

On August 7, 1974, as Mr. Nixon met in the Lincoln Sitting Room with Secretary of State Henry Kissinger, a Jew, he revealed his plan. Together the former Quaker and the Jew knelt for prayer—hard prayer.

Two days later, facing the possibility of impeachment charges, Richard Nixon went on television and resigned as President of the United States "for the sake of the office," the only President to do so without completing an elected term.

One can only wonder if, like the Old Testament character Job, Richard Nixon will rise out of the ashes to yet another victory.

GERALD RUDOLPH FORD

Gerald Rudolph Ford

THIRTY-EIGHTH PRESIDENT, 1974–1977

"For myself and for our nation, I want to thank my predecessor for all
he has done to heal our land."
> —*First words of President Carter's inaugural address, 1977*

"Mr. Vice President," intoned Chief Justice Warren Burger,
"are you prepared to take the oath of office as President of the
United States?"

As the country was reeling over the confusion of the past
few days, sharing their anxiety was the man who was about to
grasp the reins of responsibility left dangling by another. For
the first time in history, a President had resigned as America's
Chief Executive.

Less than thirteen hours earlier, President Richard Nixon
had told a national television audience, "In turning over
direction of the government to Vice President Ford, I know, as
I told the nation when I nominated him for that office ten
months ago [to replace Spiro T. Agnew, who had resigned],
that the leadership of America will be in good hands."

Now, at noon, Eastern Daylight Time, on August 9, 1974,
in the East Room of the White House, which was packed with
reporters, friends, and government officials, and with his wife,
Betty, at his side, Vice President Gerald R. Ford raised his right
hand and placed his left on a Bible opened to Proverbs 3:5–6,
which read, "Trust in the Lord with all thine heart; and lean
not unto thine own understanding. In all thy ways acknowl-
edge him, and he shall direct thy paths." It was Mr. Ford's

favorite passage of scripture, one he repeated every night as a prayer.

The brief inaugural address that followed held more religious overtones. "As we bind up the internal wounds of Watergate," he said, "let us restore the Golden Rule to our political process, and let brotherly love purge our hearts of suspicion and hate."

For Gerald Ford, religious observance was not for official ceremonies only but was an important dimension of his life.

His mother and stepfather, whose name he had been given (his mother divorced his father when Ford was an infant), were staunch Episcopalians in Grand Rapids, Michigan. Gerald Ford and his bride, Betty, were married there in Grace Episcopal Church. When they moved to Washington, Betty taught Sunday school at Immanuel Church; young Gerald was active in men's clubs.

His religious observances took on other dimensions. For example, he was a regular attender of weekly congressional prayer breakfasts. He also befriended a feisty Michigan clergyman, the Reverend Billy Zeoli, president of Gospel Films. Zeoli, who conducted chapel services for the Detroit Tigers baseball club, carried a message of positive enthusiasm about the message of Christianity—one that Gerald Ford welcomed, especially during the turbulent sixties when many in the nation were bent on striking out at all organizations, including the church.

On December 6, 1973, immediately after becoming Vice President, Gerald Ford visited the Prayer Room of the Capitol for private meditation. It was in this same room that he, while Vice President, and even after assuming the duties of President, along with four regulars (the others were Representative John Rhodes of Arizona, Representative Charles Goodell of New York, former Secretary of Defense Melvin Laird of Wisconsin, and Representative Albert Quie of Minnesota), met at noon for fifteen minutes every Wednesday. Together, they prayed for the blessings of God upon this nation and upon themselves.

"Gerald Ford had no parade of piety," said former Chaplain of the Senate Edward Elson. "He was genuine beyond reproach, a 'working Episcopalian' who wasn't ashamed to put his faith into practice."

Public worship was not uncommon for both Congressman and Mrs. Ford. Along with friends and neighbors they had gotten to know during their twenty-five years in Washington, they had joined Immanuel Church on the Hill in Alexandria, Virginia, where their children were baptized. During Mr. Ford's brief term as President, he and Betty attended St. John's Episcopal Church in Lafayette Square for Sunday morning services.

"At times," said the Reverend Peter M. Larsen, assistant pastor of St. John's, "Mr. Ford would slip into the eight o'clock morning worship almost unnoticed by the twenty or thirty others present."

Chaplain Elson observed, "President Gerald Ford was unassuming and genuinely honest in his politics. He once said to me, 'You have to give a little, take a little, to get what you really want. But you don't have to give up your principles.'"

His principles, according to some analysts, led to his defeat in the 1976 election. Just one month following his inauguration, Mr. Ford granted former President Nixon a "full, complete, and absolute pardon" for all federal crimes he might have committed as Chief Executive.

It was a rough decision which, according to President Ford, he did not treat lightly. On the day he made the decision, he attended St. John's Episcopal Church across the street from the White House to pray for guidance and understanding. He received Holy Communion and returned to the Oval Office, where he made the announcement that would have such a powerful impact on his future.

The grumbling never ceased after that Sunday morning.

The Prayer Room in the U.S. Capitol. Gerald Ford used it as a retreat.
Courtesy the Capital Historical Society.

Potential supporters fell away and the pardon became a major campaign issue for the Democrats and their front-runner, Jimmy Carter, who won the election in 1976.

Although he acknowledged that his granting of the pardon was not in his best interests politically, Gerald Ford did not regret his decision.

"I only did what I thought was right," he said.

JAMES EARL CARTER

James Earl Carter

THIRTY-NINTH PRESIDENT, 1977–1981

"Washington, D.C., is now the only city in the world where someone can call 'Dial-a-prayer' and get the White House."

—*Comedian Bob Hope*

"For Jimmy Carter, the church is an important part of his life. My husband would be lost without it," said Rosalynn Carter on WROD's radio talk show in Daytona Beach, Florida, during the successful presidential campaign of 1975. President James Earl "Jimmy" Carter represented a type of religious conviction unknown by former tenants of the White House. Unlike many of his predecessors, whose associations with the organized church were aloof and little more than academic, President Carter (given the code name "Deacon" by the Secret Service) immersed himself in his beliefs.

As a Southern Baptist and born-again Christian, Mr. Carter was never reluctant to confess that "I am a Christian" or to take the opportunity to say, "Let me tell you what Christ means to me."

"It was the sort of thing one expected to find on Sunday mornings on little southern radio stations," wrote James Wooten, White House correspondent for *The New York Times*, "this fundamentalistic 'Brother, are you saved?' piety and zeal, but not from a man seeking such an office as he."

Strangely, it worked for Jimmy Carter. In spite of the fact that he proclaimed his faith without apology, Carter slowly climbed the ladder of success in political circles that were accustomed neither to his attitude nor to the uniquely Christian phrases he sprinkled throughout his public speeches.

He taught the adult Sunday school class in his hometown congregation in Plains, Georgia, and, while serving as governor of Georgia and as President of the United States, he delighted in the chance to witness for his faith.

Once, he seemed to carry his missionary zeal a bit too far—even in the eyes of his fellow Baptists. During the campaign of 1975–76, Mr. Carter consented to an interview to be printed in the sexually oriented *Playboy* magazine. When challenged about appearing in this type of publication, Jimmy Carter responded, "Jesus commanded, 'Go into all the world and preach the gospel.' On this basis, I granted the interview."

The published interview nearly cost him the election, for in it Carter admitted that he sometimes entertained thoughts contrary to certain biblical admonitions—that is, he sometimes looked at a woman with "lust in his heart." An honest observation for any man, assuredly, it nevertheless was one he had to defend many times.

While his innocent remark may have cost him some votes, Jimmy (as he preferred to be called) Carter did defeat the incumbent, Gerald Ford, in a close election in 1976.

Immediately thereafter, the Carter family began their search for a Baptist church in Washington as their new spiritual home. But here the political overtones of the presidency prevailed. Which church should they select? It was not as easy a question to answer as it would first appear. There were other considerations and several alternatives. For instance, after lengthy investigation by aides and advisers, the Carters realized they had to choose a church not only to their liking but also "acceptable" to the people of the United States—one that maintained a Baptist flavor without giving the air of a camp meeting revival. In other words, the church would have to reflect a more "traditional" approach to worship.

Someone suggested that they attend a different church each

Sunday—sort of a pinball approach—but the Carters wished to be active participants in a church, not just attenders.

Eventually, they selected the First Baptist Church pastored by the Reverend Charles Trentham, a minister with an appreciation for liturgical worship while at the same time having earned the reputation of a devoted Southern Baptist.

Even in the expression of religion through public worship, the office of the presidency is confining. Monday morning editions of newspapers throughout the nation often carried photos of the President with captions of this nature:

> President Carter is shown with a Bible tucked under his arm, leading his family to church for worship, where they sit in the sixth row of pews, right side, and together listen to Pastor Trentham—a man with whom the President has become close. Whenever possible, Mr. Carter picks up where he left off in Plains, Georgia, and conducts the adult Sunday school class.

President Carter's first years in office were marked with a sharp focus on "moral imperatives." On both the national and the international scenes, he insisted on upholding the value of human rights. As syndicated columnist Jack Anderson observed, "Carter can see and smell the Atlanta ghetto where he once worked as a lay Baptist. . . . He can feel the impoverished Indian village where his mother labored as a Peace Corps volunteer. He identifies with those who need succor."

On the domestic scene, President Carter's close association with religion became the subject of criticism in some roundabout ways. When he urged widespread reform that might mean higher taxes for many citizens, one Republican Congressman chided, "The trouble with Carter is he's listening only to God—and God doesn't pay taxes."

Although Jimmy Carter was a faithful member of the Southern Baptist denomination, he broke with its tradition when he openly supported civil rights. He made waves among many of his fellow parishioners when he sought racial equality for African Americans. This was not something people

President Carter leaving Zion Baptist Church with the Rev. Martin Luther King, Sr. Courtesy Religious News Service.

expected—especially from a Southerner. But the President was convinced that he was doing the right thing. In a 1987 interview with author Richard Hutcheson, President Carter said, "The country at that time was searching for someone who would publicly profess a commitment to truth and integrity and the adherence to moral values—concerning peace, human rights, the alleviation of suffering—and I put forward these concepts, which are very deeply ingrained in my own character and motivations."

As he served his four years as President, it was easy for the nation to see that the church meant more to President Carter than a place for a once-a-week visit. Sophisticated theological works were part of his regular reading. Books by theologians Reinhold Niebuhr and Søren Kierkegaard—normally found only on the shelves of clergymen and seminary students— were among his favorites. He quoted from them freely, even in his speeches to the American people. This caused some historians to label Carter as the most theologically literate President since Woodrow Wilson. At the same time, the President felt himself to be a student of theology, rather than an expert.

All the theology in the world was unable to ensure him longevity in office. The man who was elected to office amid the triumphant shouts of some conservative Christians that "one of us is in the White House," was soundly defeated in his bid for reelection, partly because of a well-organized and heavily financed campaign led by ultraconservatives who felt the President had abandoned his principles. Many of the same faithful who applauded his victory in 1976 jumped ship and joined the ranks of his opponent, Ronald Reagan, in 1980, who they felt better served the cause of the Moral Majority, named and led by popular evangelist Jerry Falwell.

Today the former president works with missionary enthusiasm, still convinced he can make a difference. A small black Bible is one of the few items on the desk in his office in the Carter Center, on a hilltop overlooking Atlanta. One week each year he and "Rosie" (his affectionate nickname for his wife) volunteer for Habitat for Humanity. In June 1990 they lived out of a tent on a remote hillside in Tijuana, Mexico, building low-cost housing for those who otherwise would be homeless.

How history will rate President Carter is yet unknown. His ability to influence Congress will not be noted as one of his strong points. Unlike predecessors like Lyndon Johnson, who manipulated senators and legislators with ease, Jimmy Carter found dealing with Capitol Hill difficult, and his battles more often than not were futile. Ironically, his close association with the organized church could have been the chief contributor to this record.

As a Sunday school teacher and a lay leader within the Baptist church, Jimmy Carter was trained to say, "Present the truth, and men will follow." But Congress is not persuaded that way, and President Carter found it difficult to exchange the posture of church leader for that of a political persuader.

What Rosalynn Carter said was true. For Jimmy Carter, the church was an important part of his life, perhaps even more important than the presidency itself.

RONALD WILSON REAGAN

Ronald Wilson Reagan

FORTIETH PRESIDENT, 1981–1989

"There are times when I'm in church I think God might recognize the magnitude of my responsibility and give me an extra portion of his grace . . . and I don't feel guilty for feeling that way."

He rode to office, in one of the greatest landslides in political history, on the shoulders of an ultraconservative wing of the Christian church known as the Moral Majority. Ronald Reagan, former film actor and former governor of California, convinced the American public that he, not Jimmy Carter, would be able to get the nation back on its feet—politically, economically, and spiritually.

On what could be described as one of the most patriotic days in American history, President Reagan's first inauguration in 1981 was but part of a bizarre set of events akin to the plot of a Hollywood B movie. Those who were there or who watched on television will remember the beaming President-elect sitting beside a weary President Carter, whose face was drawn, almost void of emotion. To the podium stepped Mr. Reagan's confidant and friend, the Reverend Donn D. Moomaw, who echoed the drama of the day in his inaugural prayer:

> We thank you for the release of the hostages and for all those who made it possible. In this moment of new beginnings our hearts beat with a cadence of pride in our country and hope in its future.

For the last 444 days of the Carter administration, fifty-two Americans were held hostage in Iran as a result of the seizure of the American Embassy by alleged Iranian students. Despite diplomatic attempts to convince the Iranians to "let our people go," nothing happened. A bungled military attack backfired. Americans were growing increasingly impatient and embarrassed as television newsman Walter Cronkite ended each nightly broadcast reminding the nation just how many days up to that point the fifty-two had been in captivity.

Viewed by some as a final slap in the face of President Carter, Iran waited to free the hostages until just hours before the new President took his oath of office on the west steps of the Capitol.

As the Mormon Tabernacle Choir sang *The Battle Hymn of the Republic* and bands paraded by, American flags seemed to fly a bit higher than ever. Many observers felt a sense of renewed pride. They believed the new President had already established himself as a world leader who would make things happen. And happen they did.

The first few months of the Reagan administration were marked with cutbacks in domestic spending, elimination of social programs, tax-cut proposals, and a bold effort to get the nation back on its feet through private enterprise. Ronald Reagan left no doubt in anyone's mind that he was in charge.

But in Ronald Reagan's spiritual life, God maintained control. "I've always believed that there is a certain divine scheme of things," he once said, shortly after being elected governor of California. "I'm not quite able to explain how my election happened or why I'm here, apart from believing it is a part of God's plan for me." Later he added, "Faith in God is absolutely essential if a person is to do his best. Sometimes we're afraid to let people know that we rely on God. Taking this stand seems to be a logical and proper way to begin."

According to President Reagan, both man and God are partners in a synergistic approach to life. "There is nothing automatic about God's will," he said. "I think it is very plain that we are given a certain control of our destiny because we have a chance to choose. We are given a set of rules or guidelines in the Bible by which to live, and it is up to us to decide whether we will abide by them or not."

Ronald Reagan's continual interest in the Bible and theology were due in part to the dynamic leadership of the man to whom he referred as "my pastor," the Reverend Donn Moomaw. Moomaw, a former UCLA football star, was pastor of Bel-Air Presbyterian Church in Los Angeles. Although the President was raised as a member of the Christian Church (Disciples of Christ), he had adopted this Presbyterian congregation as his own.

"It was love at first sight—or sound," explained Ronald Reagan. "We never listen to Donn that we don't feel richer for it. I can't recall when I've looked forward to going to church more. I guess my expectation comes from knowing I'll come away inspired."

In a letter dated February 25, 1981, Moomaw wrote about the most famous member of his flock: "I know the President as a man of faith in God. He is a man without guile and a very principled man."

Unlike some of his predecessors, President Reagan never flinched from telling others about what and in whom he believed. One day he and Evangelist Billy Graham discussed, in depth, the biblical prophecy concerning the Second Coming of the Christ. According to those who heard the dialogue, Mr. Reagan held his own with the evangelist.

"After that conversation," said Mr. Reagan, "I asked Donn to send some more material on prophecies so I could check them out in the Bible for myself. You know, I was raised on the Bible. I also taught it for a long time in Sunday school."

Once when Christmas carolers serenaded then Governor Reagan in the rotunda of the State Capitol in Sacramento, California, he said to them, "My greetings are for those of all faiths, including those who believe Jesus was merely a great teacher and those who, like me, believe he is the promised Messiah, the Son of God."

Perhaps our most revealing insight into the President's faith centers in the "creed" he expressed several times:

> I believe that whatever has happened to me, whatever I've accomplished or attained, I could not have done without God's help.
>
> I believe that if I ever forget that part of my faith, if I ever forget what he has done or if I begin thinking I'm able to do something without his help, the blessings of faith will disappear as fast as an early snow.
>
> I simply believe that if you put your faith in God and ask for strength and wisdom to do what has to be done and at the same time do your best to do what you believe is right, you will be given the strength and wisdom to do it.

The President applied this creed to other personal dimensions of his life. In a valentine he wrote in 1981 to his wife, Nancy, he confessed he loved her "because you shared with me the belief that prayer and religion are private, but so vital and needed in all faiths and creeds at this time."

Perhaps the most revealing insight into President Reagan's faith came on March 30, 1981, when he was struck by a bullet fired by a would-be assassin. Donn Moomaw recalled that, upon hearing the news, he left immediately for Washington and the White House. Mrs. Reagan asked him to join her in the hospital that evening.

The President, said Moomaw, was still weak from surgery earlier that day. The bullet missed his heart by only one inch.

"Ron," asked Moomaw, "if the bullet had taken you, would you have been okay with God?"

"Yes," answered the President without hesitation.

"How do you know?" asked Moomaw.

The President looked him squarely in the eye and said, "I have a Savior."

A few days later, according to his autobiography entitled *An American Life*, the President wrote in his diary, "Whatever happens now, I owe my life to God and will serve him in every way I can."

The attempt on President Reagan's life may have been a time for proclaiming his personal faith, yet without a doubt it curtailed his habit of attending church. In 1984 a reporter asked him if he would attend church that next Sunday. The reporter quoted some Democrats who claimed that Ronald Reagan talked a lot about religion but was not seen in church.

The President admitted this was true. "I represent too much of a threat to too many other people for me to be able to go to church," he said. Then he added, "And frankly, I miss it very much."

Donn Moomaw felt that Ronald Reagan's religious convictions were "more experiential than intellectual." Experience convinced Ronald Reagan that he had a mission of sorts, and that he, like the rest of us, had some part to play in God's plan. In a pointed letter to the mother of a handicapped boy, he wrote:

> God has a plan for each one of us. Some with little faith and even less testing seem to miss in their mission, or else we perhaps fail to see their imprint on the lives of others. But bearing what we cannot change and going on with what God has given us, confident there is a destiny, somehow seems to bring a reward we wouldn't exchange for any other.

Much like the posture taken by Abraham Lincoln, who sat in the Oval Office more than a hundred years before him, Ronald Reagan was not one who longed to unite with a particular congregation. Instead, his religion was more of a personal conviction based on Christian teachings. But even more than Mr. Lincoln, President Reagan was not unwilling to confess his belief in Jesus Christ as his Savior.

GEORGE HERBERT WALKER BUSH

George Herbert Walker Bush

FORTY-FIRST PRESIDENT, 1989–

"To this day, like every parent who has lost a child, we wonder why; yet we know that, whatever the reason, she is in God's loving arms."
—*On the death of his three-year-old daughter, 1953*

"There are no atheists in foxholes or airplane cockpits." So goes an old military cliché. And anyone who has ever been in either of these situations can attest to the accuracy of the statement. President George Bush is no exception.

As a Navy pilot during World War II, the young lieutenant was shot down in the Pacific. Ever since that memorable day, he has spoken boldly about his faith in Almighty God.

This is not to imply that the life-threatening incident was a conversion experience for George Bush. Religious teaching was always a part of his home life. Either his mother, Dorothy Walker Bush, or father, Prescott Sheldon Bush, read a Bible lesson to young George and the rest of the family each morning at the breakfast table. "We regularly attended at Christ Church (Episcopalian) in Greenwich, Connecticut," he wrote in his autobiography, *Looking Forward*.

George Bush's religious convictions were never more tested than in 1953 when his three-year-old daughter, Robin, was diagnosed as suffering from leukemia. She died six months later. "Prayer had always been an important part of our lives," recalls the President, "but never more so than during those six months. Barbara and I sustained each other; but in the end, it was our faith that truly sustained us, as, gradually but surely,

Robin slipped away. To this day, like every parent who has ever lost a child, we wonder why; yet we know that, whatever the reason, she is in God's loving arms."

A few months later, Mr. Bush told the junior high Sunday school class he taught that young Robin's death was just one example of the mysterious will of God.

The sovereignty of God—the view that nothing happens without God's knowledge—has dominated the personal theology of George Bush. Consequently, his presidency has been one in which he insists that his staff reflect the highest in moral standards.

Unlike his predecessor, President Bush is not shy about attending public worship. The former vestryman of St. Anne's Episcopal Church in Kennebunkport, Maine, has kept a strong relationship with a variety of congregations—particularly with St. Martin's Episcopal Church in Houston, Texas, and Washington's National Cathedral, where he currently holds membership. In fact, President Bush still counts September 29, 1990, as one of the highlights of his presidency, when he presided at the final stone-laying ceremony of the cathedral.

On the surface, President Bush appears to be a spokesman for the fundamentalist right-wing element of the Christian church. His conservative stance on abortion, women's rights, and civil rights seems to be right out of the pages of a textbook written by Jerry Falwell or Pat Robertson. During the campaign of 1988, he told a reporter that he was "born-again." Yet he did admit he felt awkward using such terms and that he normally did not speak the language of the so-called evangelicals.

Interpretation of language was not necessary on that memorable evening of January 16, 1991, when America launched into the war in the Persian Gulf called Desert Storm. As a United Nations deadline for Iraq to withdraw from Kuwait was about to expire, President Bush telephoned Presiding Bishop Edmond Browning of the Episcopal Church and U.S.

Senate Chaplain Richard Halverson and told them he had been praying for peace. Both prayed with him on the phone.

On Wednesday, January 16, Bush called Evangelist Billy Graham. "I need you," he said. Graham, a long-time personal friend, arrived at the White House at about 5:45 P.M. Allied planes were already heading for Baghdad. Throughout the evening, the evangelist prayed five times, both with Bush alone and with other members of the family.

The next day, at the White House, the President told congressional leaders, "There's a lot of prayer going on here, on Capitol Hill and across this whole country. And it will be that way until this [war] is concluded."

Desert Storm was over quickly—exactly one hundred hours after the ground war began. Yet during this short time, quite possibly more prayers were offered by Americans than at any time in history, and the loudest "Amens" came from the White House.

And so George Bush, like the thirty-nine men before him who placed their hands on a Bible and swore to "faithfully execute the office of the President of the United States," tries to uphold an individual sense of values without offending those whom he was pledged to serve.

When the weight of responsibility takes its toll, when the tension mounts to a height greater than anyone should have to bear, when one crisis after another looms at the door of the Oval Office, for George Herbert Walker Bush, the oath with which he began his presidency will become more pronounced as his daily prayer:

"So help me God."

Presidential Church Affiliations

(listed by denomination)

BAPTIST (3)

J. Carter
W. Harding
H. Truman

CONGREGATIONALIST (1)

C. Coolidge

DISCIPLES OF CHRIST (3)

J. Garfield
L. Johnson
R. Reagan

EPISCOPAL (8)

G. Bush
G. Ford
J. Madison
J. Monroe
F. Pierce
F. Roosevelt
J. Tyler
G. Washington

METHODIST (2)

W. McKinley
J. Polk

PRESBYTERIAN (6)

J. Buchanan
G. Cleveland
D. Eisenhower
B. Harrison
A. Jackson
W. Wilson

QUAKER (2)

H. Hoover
R. Nixon

REFORMED (2)

T. Roosevelt
M. Van Buren

ROMAN CATHOLIC (1)

J. Kennedy

UNITARIAN (4)

J. Adams
J. Q. Adams
M. Fillmore
W. Taft

UNAFFILIATED (8)

C. Arthur
U. Grant
W. Harrison
R. Hayes
T. Jefferson
A. Johnson
A. Lincoln
Z. Taylor

Note on Research

The author spent years researching the material for this book. As a graduate of Capital University with a major in American History and after completing requirements for his Ph.D. in Communications at Michigan State University (with a concentration on the speaking styles of American Presidents), he is familiar with the expressions of faith uttered by those who occupy the Oval Office.

In addition, the author has visited presidential libraries throughout this nation in search of records that reveal insights into the religious affiliations of the Presidents. He has also interviewed those who were willing to share their observations about the Presidents they knew. Those with whom he spoke include: Mr. Clement Conger, former curator of the White House; Dr. Richard Halverson, chaplain of the U.S. Senate; Senator Paula Hawkins; Dr. Edward L. R. Elson, former chaplain of the Senate; and various clergymen of the churches attended by the Presidents.